Chinese
Palmistry

First published by Orion Forlag in 2001
© Vega 2003
Text © Henning Hai Lee Yang 2003

ISBN 1-84333-740-1

A catalogue record for this book is available from the British Library

Published in 2003 by
Vega
Chrysalis Books
The Chrysalis Building
Bramley Road
London W10 6SP
Visit our website at www.chrysalisbooks.co.uk

An imprint of **Chrysalis** Books Group plc

Editor: Lisa Morris
Design: Andrew Sutterby
Jacket design: Roland Codd
Jacket illustration: Shahid Mahood
Managing Editor: Laurence Henderson
Production: Susan Sutterby

Printed in Great Britain by CPD Wales

Chinese
Palmistry

A Guide to the Ancient Oriental Art of Hand Reading

HENNING HAI LEE YANG

Henning Hai Lee Yang was born in the year of the Ox and says that he is doomed to work hard all the time, like so many others born under the same astrological sign. He has always been interested in the art of Chinese fortune-telling and can trace his family back over a thousand years to the legendary sage Yang Chiu Pu, one of China's most famous fortune-tellers. Henning specializes in Chinese and Western astrology, face reading, I Ching, Feng Shui and palmistry.

Vega titles by the same author

Mian Xiang: The Chinese Art of Face Reading
The Year of the Horse
The Year of the Goat

Contents

Introduction

The Ancient Greeks, Egyptians, Romans and Indians all recognized hand reading as a way to foretell the future. But it was the Chinese who really developed the technique. It has been taught in China since the beginning of the Warring States period (475–221 BCE) and is considered to be a form of science, which was first recorded by being carved on to bamboo flakes.

Chinese Palmistry is meant to be a simple and practical guide to this fascinating art that will provide you with enough information for you to use it to analyse people. It has taken me many years to collect the valuable insights in this book. I hope they will bring much enjoyment to everyone interested in the ancient art of Chinese palmistry.

THE TEACHINGS OF
CHINESE HAND READING

In China the ancient tradition of hand reading is a very powerful tool for revealing details of a person's character, health, past and future. Some Western doctors and psychologists have also applied hand-reading techniques when making diagnoses.

One thing that differentiates the Chinese technique from the Western technique is gender. In Chinese palmistry the left hand is reserved for the man, while the right hand is reserved for the woman. Thus the principles of Yin and Yang are also taken into account. In my experience this is essential, because I have noticed that the feminine side of a person is more prominent in the right hand, while the masculine side tends to be more striking in the left hand.

In this book I have made around 200 analyses, which are more or less based on the five main lines and eight mounts defined on the palm of the hand. (Mounts are the fleshy bumps that signify the degree of influence of a particular planet, such as the mount of Mars – see pages 11-13.) Each interpretation has its own explanation and illustration. It is important to remember that the lines will change according to age and way of life; your hands cannot hide very much about you. But your life is not destined in advance. If your hands show some negative tendencies, you can always do something about it. The hand can even act as a tool of advance warning.

In my years of research I have found that there are always stumbling blocks, or shall we say some dramatic changes, for humans at the following ages: 18 years, 30 years, 45 years, 55 years and 63 years. These turning points in our life seem to be of great importance to every one of us. We are destined to make these changes, whether we like it or not, but if we are prepared, we can steer away from great upheavals and difficulties.

HOW TO READ THE HAND

HAND TYPE

A soft and delicate hand

This implies a cultivated and sensitive person, who also might be rather lazy and materialistic. They want to enjoy life without having to make any effort.

A thick and elastic hand

This shows a very artistic person, who is also intelligent and business-minded. They know how to achieve wealth and success.

A rugged and rigid hand

This belongs to a person who enjoys doing a lot of physical work. They tend to be practical and simple-minded people with a methodical approach to life.

A strong and compact hand

This indicates a very stubborn person with a strong will and lots of perseverance – they will do anything to reach their goal.
They can be very ambitious, with a tendency to be self-centred, which makes them many enemies.

MOUNTS OF THE PALM

The Chinese have their own expressions for the different mounts of the palm. Usually they apply terms from *I Ching* (Book of Changes) as follows: Ken, Zheng, Xun, Li, Shen, Tui, Chien and Hum. The middle of the hand is called Ming Tang, or the House of the Sun and the Moon. Many of these terms actually correspond to the Western style of palm reading.

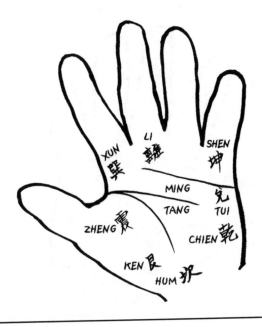

Planetary Names of the Mounts

Ken corresponds to the mount of Venus, which indicates a good appreciation and understanding of all that is beautiful and satisfying. A well-developed mount reveals a person that is both artistic and creative.
Zheng corresponds to the lower mount of Mars, which indicates self-restraint, endurance and self-defence. If the mount is well developed it shows a person with an enormous fighting spirit. If flat, it reveals a very indecisive person.

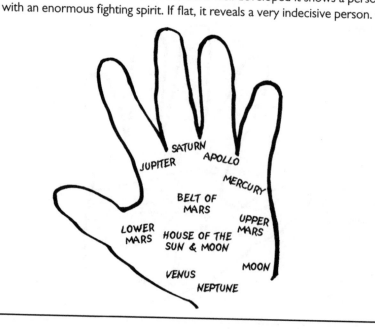

Xun corresponds to the mount of Jupiter, which indicates power and ambition. A well-developed mount reveals ambition and a strong desire to succeed in life. A flat mount means the opposite.

Li corresponds to the mount of Saturn, which indicates diligence, good judgement and virtue. A well-developed mount shows someone who is reasonable, principled and hardworking. A flat mount indicates the opposite. In Chinese palmistry, the mount of Li is placed both under the middle finger and the ring finger *(see illustration of the mounts of the palm, p. 11)*. I will refer to both locations as sites for the mount of Li in this book.

Shen corresponds to the mounts of both Apollo and Mercury. The mount of Apollo indicates recognition and fame. If it is well developed, the person can be very successful and famous; a flat mount means the opposite. The mount of Mercury indicates intelligence, flexibility and good business sense. If it is well developed, the person is very business-minded and knows how to make good money.

Tui corresponds to the upper mount of Mars, which indicates courage and strong will. If it is well developed, the person is brave and knows what they want. A flat mount reveals a coward and indecisive person.

Chien corresponds to the mount of the Moon, which indicates feelings, dreams and mystical abilities. A well-developed mount is the sign of a person who has psychic talents. A flat mount indicates someone who does not fantasize or have dreams.

Hum corresponds to the mount of Neptune, the lowest part of the palm. If it is well developed, the person is articulate, outgoing and sympathetic.

Ming Tang corresponds to the belt of Mars. If it is well developed, the person is well balanced and knows how to take care of themselves.

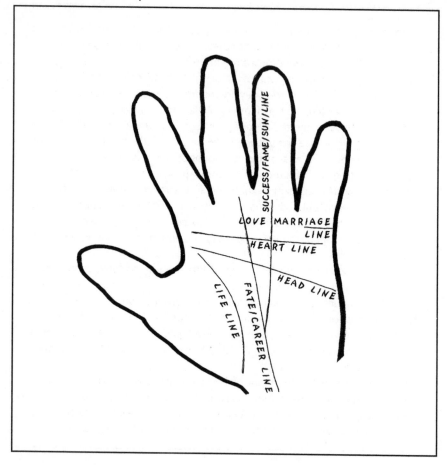

LINES OF THE PALM

There are many arguments over the accuracy of hand reading. It is common knowledge that by reading the rings on a tree trunk, it is possible to define how long the tree has lived. Dark marks on the rings indicate that the tree has been attacked by some kind of disease at that particular point in its life.

By reading the lines in your hand, you will discover much the same information. As the structure of the human body is so much more complicated than that of a tree, there are more specific lines within our hands, each with its own value and meaning. Most of the information has been gathered by fortune-tellers and even by doctors interested in this kind of science. Below you will see an illustration of a hand with the most important lines on it. They are the lines revealing your personality, your present state of life and, most importantly, your future. Remember, the Chinese analyse the left hand for a man and the right hand for a woman.

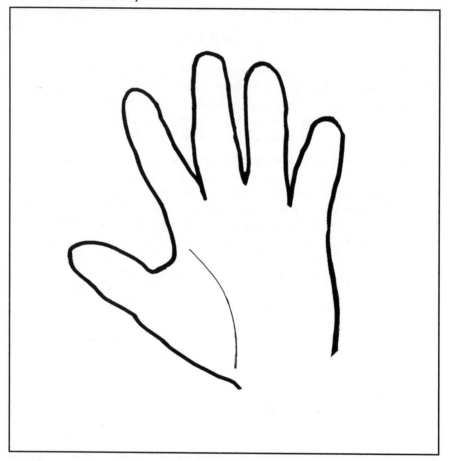

The Life Line

This line indicates longevity, vitality and quality of life. A clear, long line indicates a healthy constitution and prolonged life. A full and circular line suggests a very energetic person, while a faint line suggests someone who is lazy and inactive. As I explained earlier, though, everything can be changed. If you start to be more active, the line will become full and circular. If the line is very overlapped, or even cut, you will have to pay more attention to your lifestyle. It may be that it is too extreme and you might even experience something negative at a particular point in your life, so be careful.
Here are some analyses of life line formations and their meanings:

Lots of energy and a strong sex drive
This is indicated by a strong and clearly marked life line.

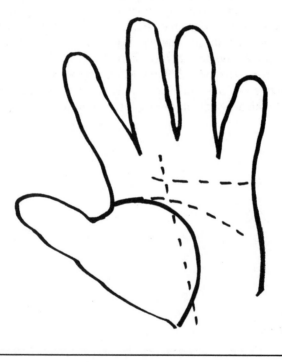

Restlessness

A life line that ends on the mount of the Moon indicates a restless and unstable person who is constantly on the move. Such an individual is adventurous, with a desire to travel and see the world.

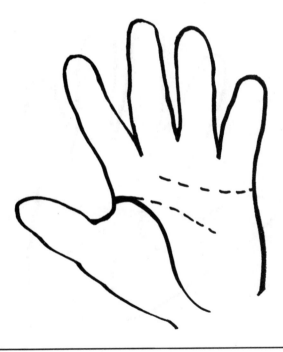

Poor and worsening health

A short life line that curves and ends on the mount of Zheng is a very bad omen, which must be taken seriously. The person should see their doctor.

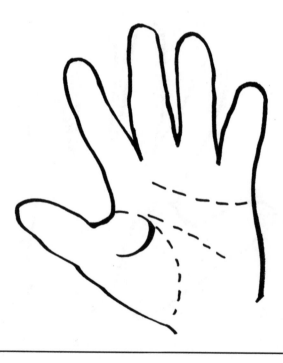

Poor health

A life line that consists of many small lines and chains shows poor health – in particular, it indicates that the lungs are not working as well as they should.

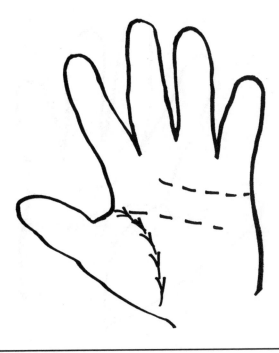

Ailing health with the possibility of recovery

A life line with a break, with the parts overlapping within short distances of each other, indicates poor fitness with a possibility of recovery. It is essential that the individual pays attention to his or her health and quickly restores it.

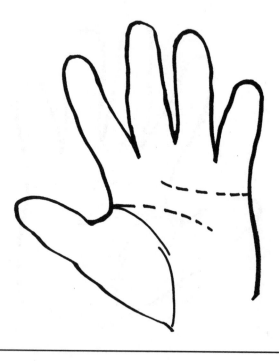

Nine lives

When the life line has breaks, with overlapping lines that have squares attached to them, it indicates several accidents. However, the squares will have a protective effect on the person – just like a cat with nine lives.

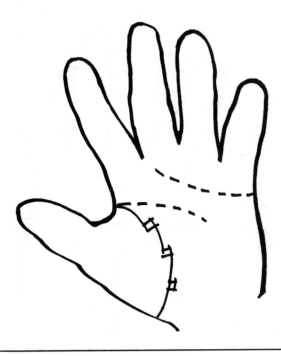

Bad health, in particular weak immunity

A poorly marked life line, chained by small crosses, is a very bad omen. It shows a depleted state of health, not least a weak immunity system. People with such a life line will easily catch colds and have several health problems. However, it is possible for them to build up the immunity system with a good diet, regular exercise and plenty of sleep.

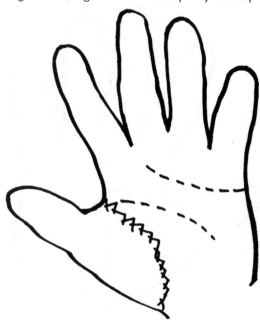

A possible accident while travelling

An obvious break on the life line does not bode well. It is important to take things easy and try not to make journeys that are too long. Accidents may lie in wait, but if the person is careful they will be avoided.

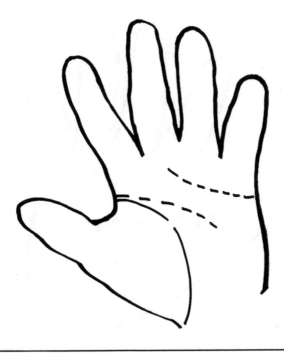

Bad health, especially in relation to the head

An island in the middle of the life line, with an attaching subsidiary line cutting the head line, indicates bad health – especially problems connected with the head region. However, with the right diet and daily exercise, recovery is possible.

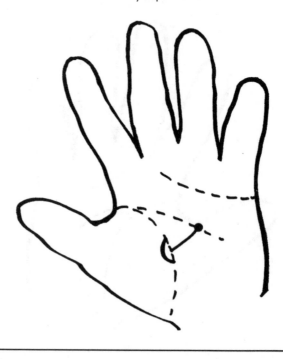

Worries about a loved one

The sudden appearance of an island close to the life line, and clearly cut by smaller lines, indicates concern for a loved one. You reflect and think too much about that person – possibly someone with poor health.

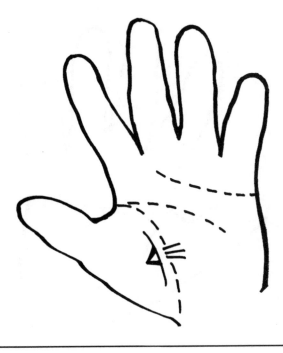

Ailing health

When a branch line cuts the life line and slopes downward towards the mount of the Moon, this is a sign of a weak person, who may have alcohol and narcotics problems.

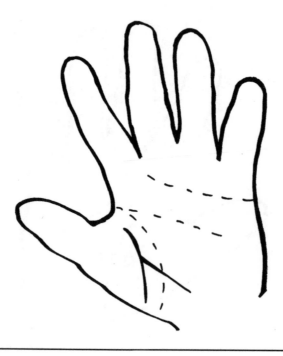

Sorrow and insecurity
A number of irregular lines appearing on the mount of Venus indicate unhappiness and lack of stability. The person feels they are inadequate and that many of their plans do not work out properly.

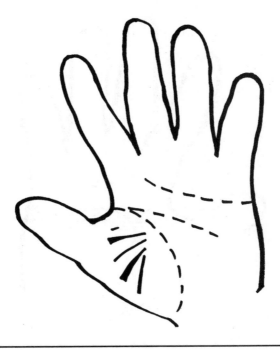

Changeable potency and lack of interest in sex

When the life line has a clear dot (A), from which arises a line with a cross at the end on the lower mount of Mars, this is a sign of fluctuating potency. If, in addition, all the small lines cut the life line, the person does not have any sexual appetite at all.

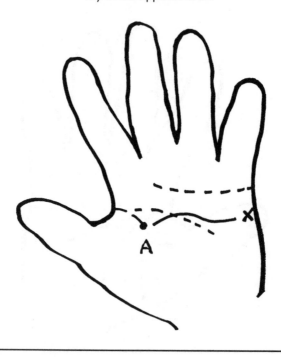

Self-destruction and a tendency to suicide

An island that appears right by the side of the life line is a sign of self-destruction and thoughts of suicide. It is also a sign that the person easily gets into a depressed state, which might give rise to thoughts of committing suicide. They should be careful not to isolate themselves.

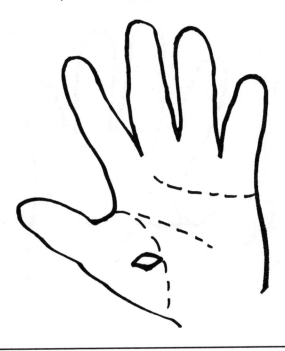

Unhappy love

An extra line beneath the life line, on the lower mount of Mars, shows a person who has fallen in love with someone who does not return that love with the same feelings. Such a relationship would be rather strenuous and difficult to maintain.

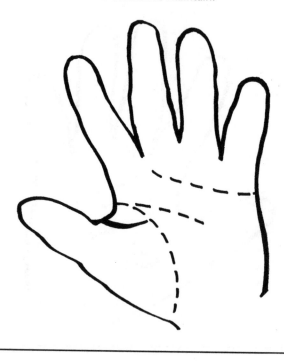

An unwilling break-up

When a star appears on a shorter line next to the life line, and an extra line connects the star with an island on the head line, the person must grudgingly leave their loved one, although they may find it hard to do so.

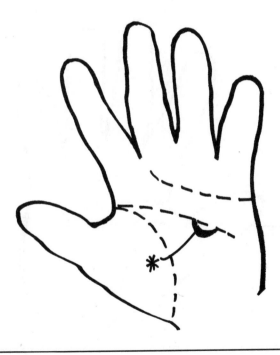

A cold and unhappy relationship
An extra short line behind the life line on the mount of Venus shows
unhappy love, or love that is on the point of dying out.

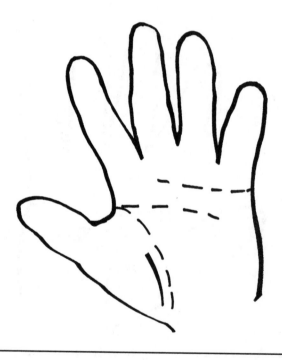

A happy and healthy relationship

An extra line running parallel with the life line is a good sign. The person can count on receiving a lot of love and having a very good relationship with their partner.

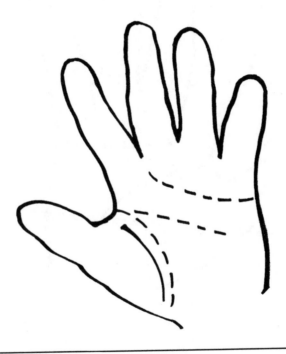

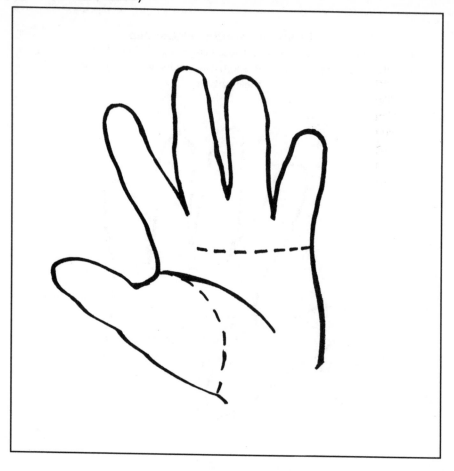

The Head Line or Intelligence Line

This line indicates reason, intelligence, memory and artistic and practical talents. The longer and more marked the line, the more intelligent the person will be. And the bigger the angle between the head line and the life line, the more practical he or she is. A horizontal line suggests an earthbound person, while a line that slopes down to the mount of the Moon represents a person with good intuition. A line that is spliced is indicative of a very creative person. Here are some analyses of head line formations and their meanings:

High intelligence

This is a sign of super-intelligence, as well as iron will. A person with this combination will go far in life, especially if they know how to make use of their talents. However, they also might be rather moody, fluctuating between loving and loathing someone. A person with such a line needs to develop tolerance.

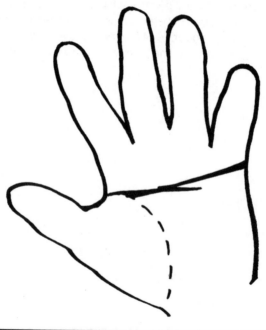

Greedy and ruthless

A head line that runs straight into the heart line shows a person who can be rather heartless and materialistic. They will be prepared to do anything for money, so they would be wise to develop a sense of generosity and be more considerate towards others.

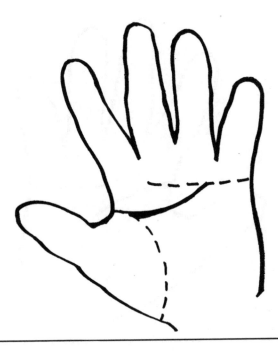

Independent and wilful

A head line that lies quite far away from the life line shows a person who likes to deal with things in their own way. Sometimes they will manage well; at other times they will not be so lucky. It is vital for such a person to seek help and accept people who are willing to assist – it will make life a lot easier.

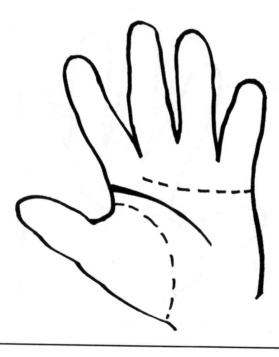

Strong self-confidence

A head line that lies close to the life line shows great independence, optimism and a good portion of self-confidence. Such a person will go far in life with this kind of attitude.

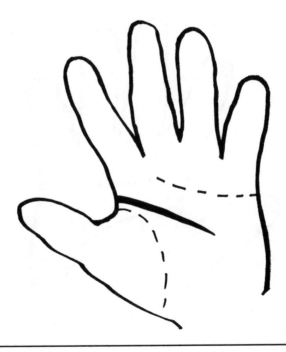

Premature old age
When there is an island at the end of the head line, that person feels much older than they really are, and they tend to age much earlier than expected. Stress and worries cause such a negative state of mind.

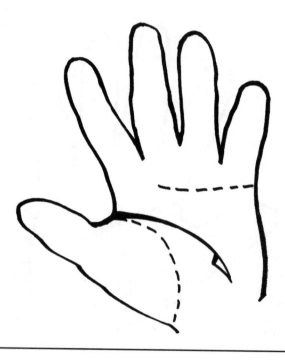

Indecisiveness

A head line that is connected to the life line, but with a lower starting point, shows a very unsettled person. This formation often occurs on the hands of women who tend to have difficulties in separating their reason from their feelings.

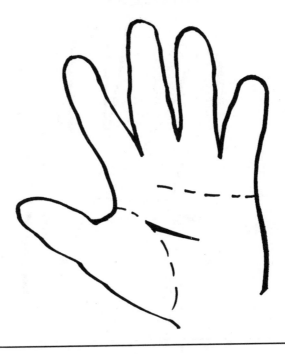

Huge self-confidence

A head line that divides into two directions, one towards the mount of Sun or the mount of Mercury and the other sloping down to the mount of Moon, is also a sign of large amounts of self-confidence. This is indicative of a person who is good at planning and organizing, and has the ability to translate their ideas into action.

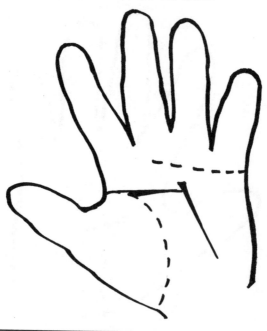

Highly respected and famous

A clear line branching out from the head line towards the index finger or mount of Jupiter shows someone held in great esteem. Such a person will be capable of achieving great things.

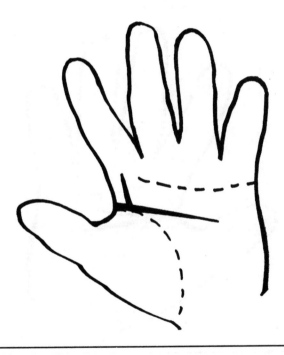

Diligence

A head line that divides into two directions, one towards the heart line and the other sloping down slightly, is a sign of a highly conscientious person. Such a person is very active and gets things done properly.

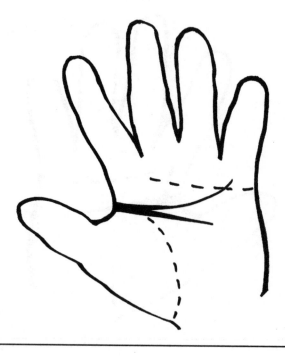

Restless and unstable without aim

A head line that is chained and divided belongs to an unsettled and unconfident person. They do not realize themselves, because they are incapable of making any decision and tend just to drift. But they can remedy this by making certain efforts to change their attitude and way of thinking.

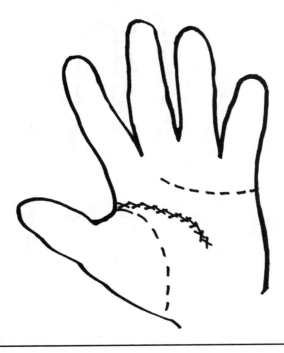

An interest in literature and writing
When the head line is divided with a white dot in the middle, it is a sign of a journalist, accomplished professional writer or productive amateur writer.

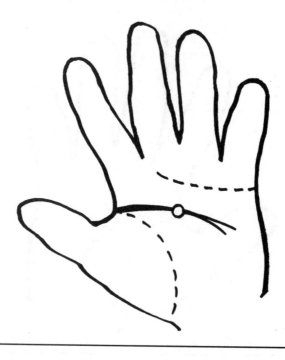

Low intelligence and a lack of common sense
A short head line indicates an immature person with poor mental capacity.
This may have been caused by the mother becoming ill, or living an
unhealthy lifestyle, during pregnancy.

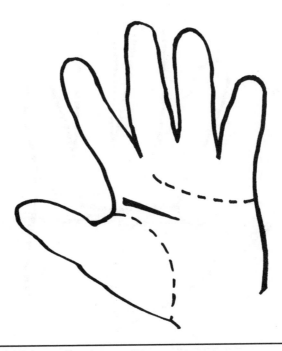

Success and recognition

An extra line arising from the head line towards the mount of Shen (mount of Mercury), beneath the little finger, is a sign of a very diligent person who has the potential to become rich and famous.

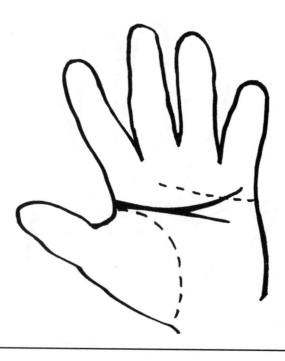

Small subsidiary lines on either side of the head line

Lines on the upper side of the head line (A) indicate favourable financial and career possibilities. Small lines occurring beneath the head line (B) and at the end of it (C) are negative signs, showing poor memory and bad health. The person should relax and pay more attention to the body and soul.

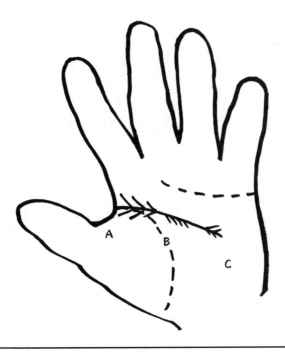

Migraine attacks
A head line that is divided into small, fine lines belongs to a person who suffers from headaches or migraines. It is also an indication of a complete lack of initiative or any goal in life.

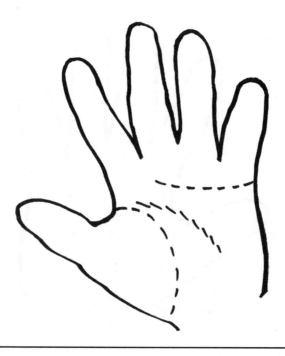

Happy and pleasant
A head line that starts quite far down on the life line shows charm and dedication. This person will be dutiful, humorous and harmonious.

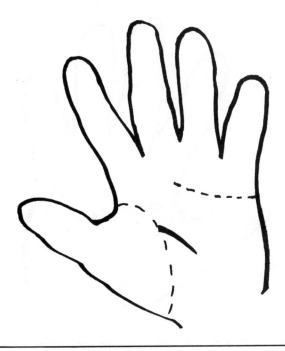

Low intelligence and poor powers of concentration

When the end of the head line is divided in this way, it shows poor concentration and little intelligence. However, with proper training these problems can be overcome.

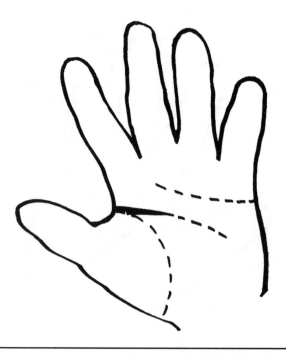

Unsatisfied in love

A double head line indicates a partner who is not satisfied with a one-on-one relationship and would like to get involved with an additional person. A threesome may result, which can make for a lot of unforeseen problems.

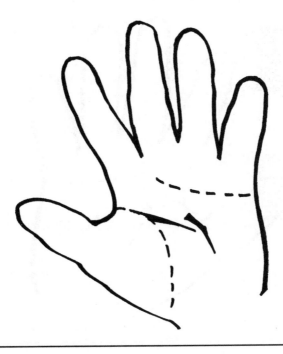

Lazy with little perseverance

When the head line suddenly bends off, it is an indication of a person who is good at starting things but lacks the endurance to fulfil the task when problems show. The person is both lazy and lacks the confidence to do things properly.

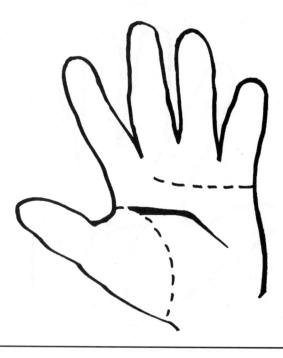

Business minded

A head line that divides in this way shows a very capable person who is good at realizing their aims in life. Unsurprisingly, this person has good business acumen and is capable of being both rich and successful.

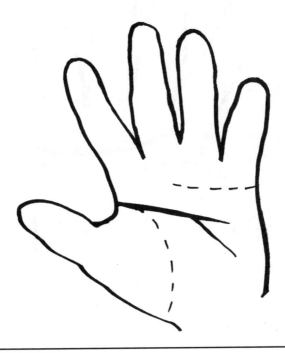

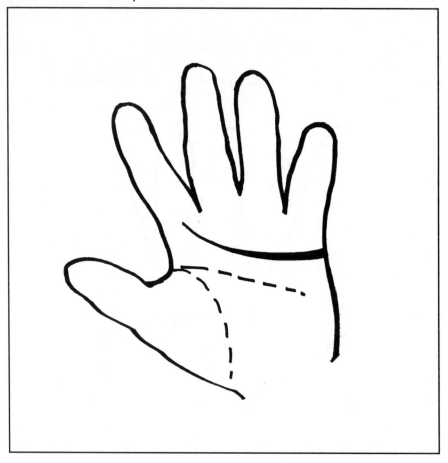

The Heart Line

This line reveals emotions and relationships, as well as physical health. A long, clear line shows a person who is intensely loving, faithful and trustworthy. A weak line indicates a sentimental person, while a short line (shorter than under your ring finger) indicates someone who is cold and independent – many freedom-loving people have this kind of line formation. Branches arising from the line suggest romantic happenings, while descending branches indicate negative experiences in love matters. A line with many small lines crossing each other shows someone who is fickle in love. A wavering line with many deep holes also indicates a weak heart, so if you have such a pattern you should watch what you eat. Avoid food with strong cholesterol content, and talk to your doctor about your blood pressure. Here are some analyses of heart line formations and their meanings:

Intense and stable in love

When the heart line bends upward and ends under the mount of Jupiter beneath the index finger, the person is faithful and stable in love. They can also be rather intense and purposeful in their pursuit of love.

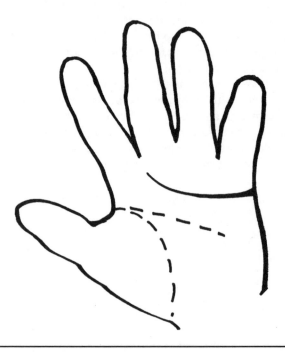

Unfeeling and unromantic

A very short heart line is a sign of someone who is cold and calculating. This person does not understand anything about love (although this attitude can be changed) and possesses a deep desire to be independent.

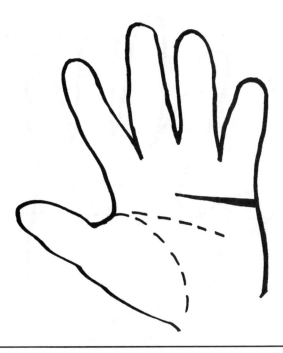

Nervous and unpredictable

When the heart line sinks down to the head line, just under the middle finger, it shows a person who is very romantic but at times also very changeable in their pursuit of love. Such an individual can be characterized as both nervous and uncertain.

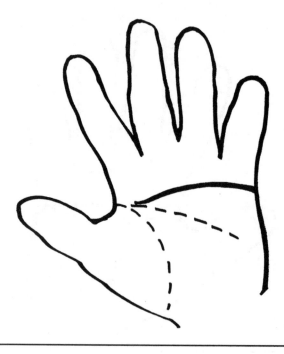

Great maturity at a young age

Two heart lines that run parallel to each other, with the first line ending just under the middle finger, indicates great maturity at a young age. Such advanced development can cause difficulties however. It is important for the person to be alert to sexual problems that may arise during this period.

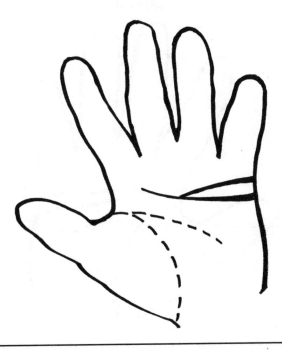

Two-sided nature

When there are two parallel heart lines running straight to the mount of Jupiter beneath the index finger, it is a sign of a split personality. The individual will be either loving and easy-going, or selfish and difficult to be with. Such a person will have a strong sexual appetite and will experience great change in their life.

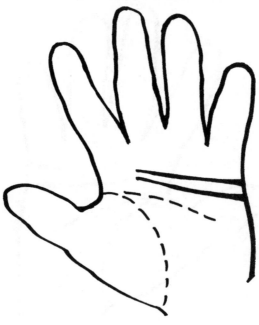

A deep and intense love

When the heart line slopes down towards the lower mount of Mars, it indicates a deep and intense love. This person is very focused on love, which will prevent them from developing other aspects of their life. Interestingly, many sensitive artists and writers often have such a line combination.

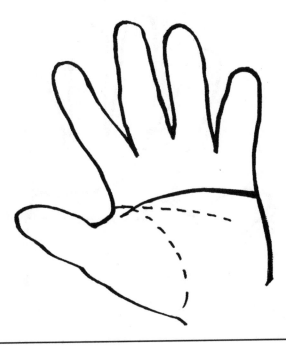

Strong selfishness

A heart line that runs down under the mount of Saturn shows a person who is egotistic and self-centred. They will have to subdue their ego in order to make life easier for themselves.

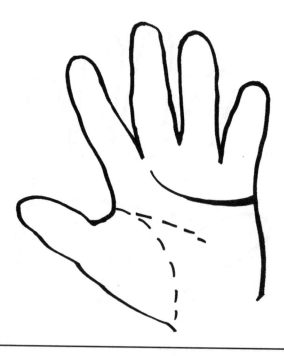

All or nothing

A heart line that runs directly towards the gap between the index finger and the middle finger indicates great intensity in love. It also means that the person will be either very demanding or want nothing at all.

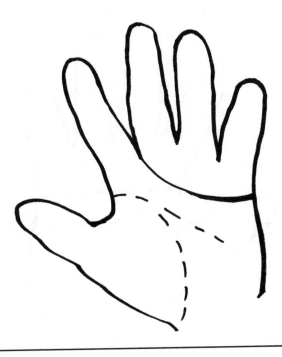

Strong, deep love, but also dangerous jealousy
When the heart line covers the whole hand, it is an indication of deep love.
But it is also an indication of possessiveness that borders on a deep and
dangerous jealousy.

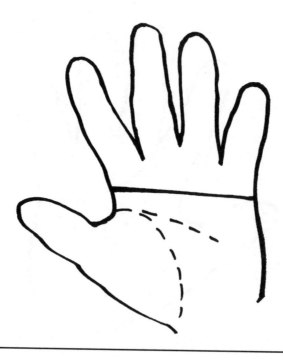

A strong sexual desire

When both the heart line and the head line are divided into chain formations, it shows a person who is very fond of sex, and only sex. They are not content with just one partner, and will constantly change partners in pursuit of new sexual experiences.

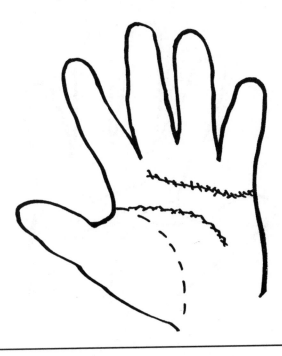

A conscientious love

When the heart line splits into two directions as shown here, it indicates a person who is very honest in love. Once they have decided to be with someone, they will be conscientious and faithful, and will never run away from their commitments.

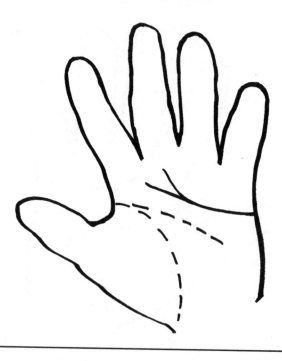

Good intuition in love matters

When there are three islands on the heart line, it is a sign of good intuition in love. This person will always know their partner's thoughts and desires.

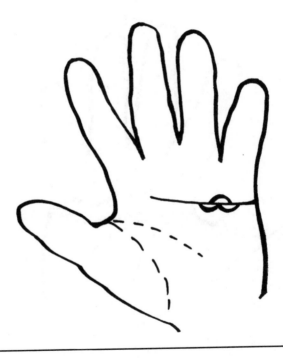

A flexible partner

A heart line that waves somewhat indicates great flexibility in love matters. Someone who has such a feature will be co-operative and reasonable, and will never let feelings take charge.

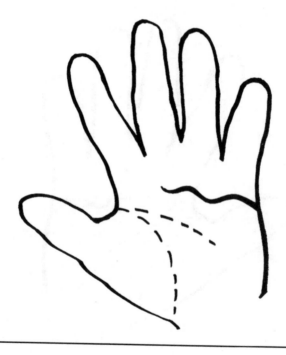

Broken love

A heart line that is separated as shown indicates a discontinued love affair. Although this is a bad omen, if the person concerned insists on doing something about such a situation, he or she will come out of it stronger for the experience.

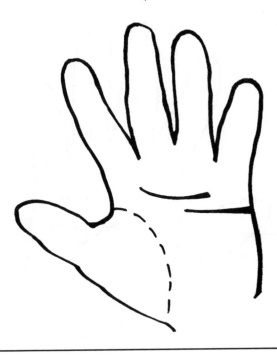

Diplomatic and eloquent

When two or three smaller lines occur at the beginning of the heart line, it is a sign of someone who is flexible, diplomatic and extremely articulate.

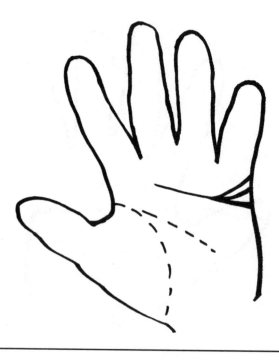

Luck in love affairs
If there are several small lines running on the upper side of the
heart line, it indicates good fortune in matters of the heart.
For this person, love is a bed of roses.

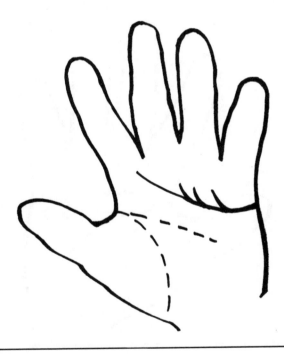

Artistic talents

This formation indicates an artistic, romantic and sensitive person. They will make great success out of creative pursuits such as writing and painting.

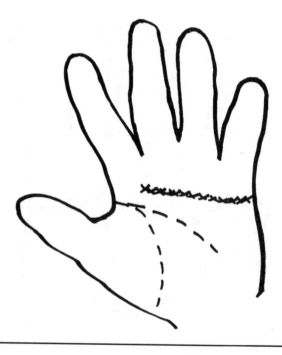

Unhappy love
This person will experience a love relationship that is struggling to flourish. They will feel misunderstood and rejected by their partner, which will make them very unhappy.

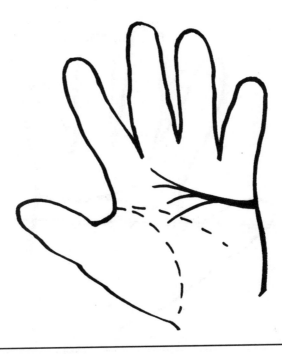

Stagnation and setbacks because of an unhappy love affair

When the heart line splits into two directions, with a sideline running towards the head line, it indicates unhappy love. The person has just experienced a period of stagnation and hopelessness, but this can be only temporary. It is wise for them to seek an easy way out of this situation.

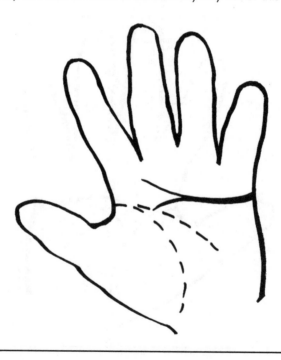

Temporary separation

An island at the end of the heart line indicates a short-term separation from your loved one, perhaps because of a serious disagreement. However, it also means that your partner is going away for a period of time in order to work in a foreign place.

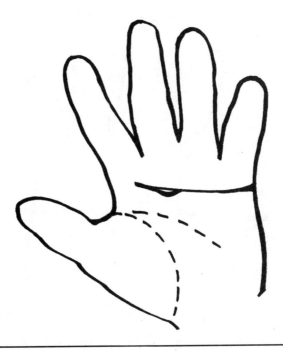

A permanent separation
A cross that appears at the end of the heart line indicates a permanent separation from your sweetheart. This is a very bad omen.

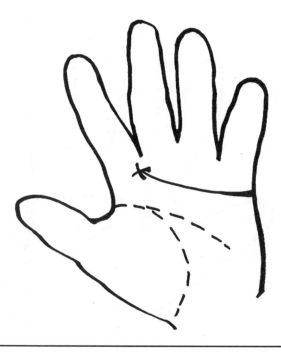

An intense flirtation or adultery

When the heart line ends with many smaller and finer lines on each side, it indicates a serious flirtation or an unstable love relationship. This is a sign of a person with strong sexual desire.

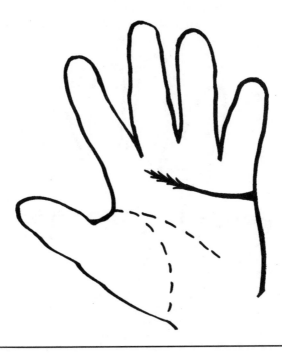

A threesome relationship

A line running between the life line and the heart line, with a star at the points at which it meets both of these lines, is a negative omen. It signifies an individual's involvement in two different relationships. Such a situation will necessarily give rise to intrigues and jealousy between the parties involved. At its worst, such a relationship will end very dramatically, and in tragedy. Luckily, however, this line can serve as an early warning: all three parties can do something about the situation before it is too late.

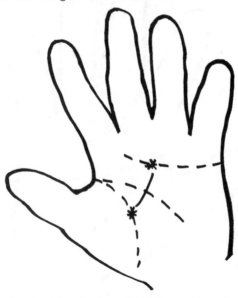

A difficult relationship involving several people

When an ordinary heart line runs towards the index finger, but there is also another minor line with an island at the beginning that runs toward the head line, this is a negative omen. It indicates a threesome that will not end happily. The minor line might even cut the head line or the life line, and the longer and deeper the cut is, the more the person will get hurt. However, there is a chance to remedy the situation. The person involved will have to make a choice instead of running two shows at the same time.

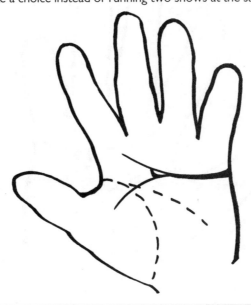

A short-lived relationship

An island underneath the heart line and beneath the ring finger does not bode well. It indicates a relationship that is not functioning properly and will not last for long. This often applies to a woman who has become someone's mistress.

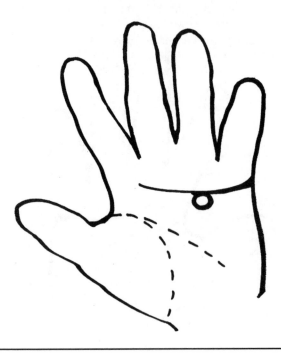

A derisory role in a relationship

When there is a square on the upper side of the heart line, it indicates that the person will not be taken seriously in a love relationship and will be treated as a joke.

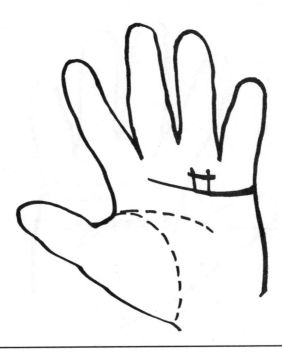

A diligent and dutiful person

When an extra line appears beneath the heart line, it shows duty, diligence and great working capacity. This is someone who is willing to sacrifice much of themselves in order to reach the top.

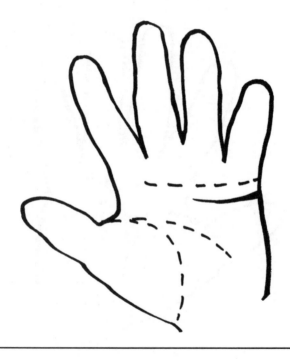

A weak and poor heart

When the heart line has small, irregular lines (A) on both sides, as well as small dots (B) blocking the line, it is an indication of a weak and dysfunctional heart. It is vital that the person takes certain precautions.

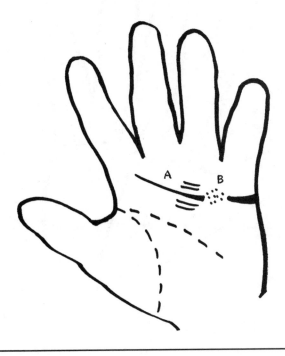

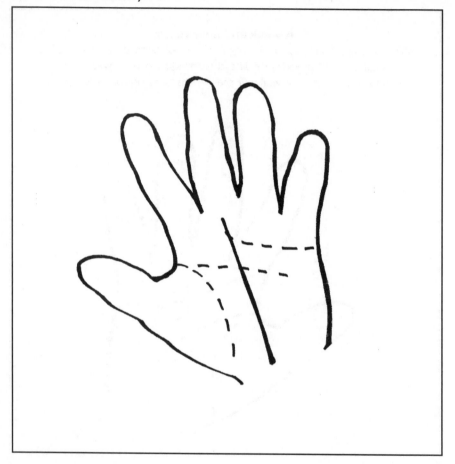

The Career Line

This line indicates career opportunities. If it is well marked and long, you can be certain you are managing your career in a positive way. A wavering line indicates an indecisive person who is always shifting jobs and career directions – every employer would be wise to check this line before they recruit anyone new. This line usually starts from a midpoint at the base of the palm and travels to the mount beneath the index finger, middle finger, ring finger or little finger. In the first case, you will obtain much power, in the second enormous success, in the third artistic fame, and in the fourth economic prosperity. Here are some analyses of career line formations and their meanings:

Lines running out from the career line

When lines arise from the career line, it is a very good omen, suggesting that the person can expect to run into better times. When the line is running towards (A), the person has great ambitions and will be successful at whatever they do. A short line running towards (B) means the person will put all their energy into a certain direction in order to reach their goal in life. A line running out towards the mount of Apollo (C), the mount between Li and Shen, means a successful career. A line running towards the mount of Mercury (D), the mount of Shen, signals good profits and economic success.

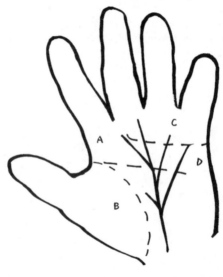

Survival of an eventual accident

A square at the end of the career line (A) means the person will survive a serious accident in the near future. A corresponding square at the bottom of the line (B) indicates someone who will manage to sort out differences in a family conflict to the mutual benefit of both parties.

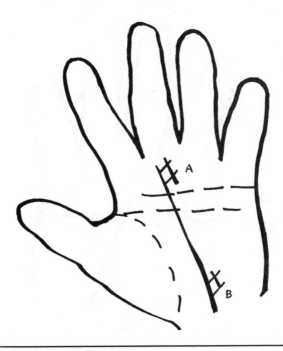

An impending accident

A cross at the end of the career line signals that an accident is about to happen, so a person with this pattern should proceed with caution.

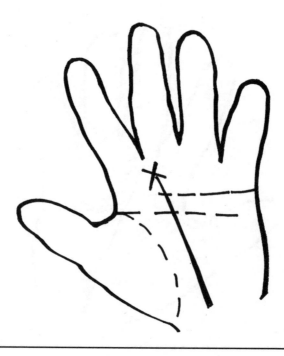

Interest in the paranormal

When the career line is cut horizontally by a line from the heart line or head line, it indicates great interest in supernatural phenomena. Most likely they will be someone with psychic powers, such as a clairvoyant.

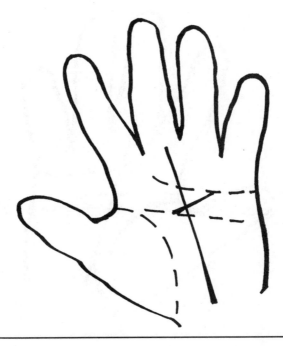

A fortified life
When the life line is very short, but the career line starts at the bottom of the hand with a greater branch, it means that the life line will be strengthened by the helping line. However, places where the lines overlap each other could signal great changes in the person's life.

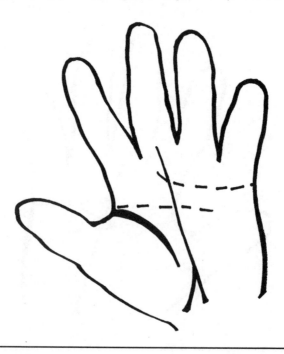

A fresh start in life

A career line that suddenly appears in the middle of the palm indicates a new start, at around 45 to 55 years old. A fresh career will certainly bring along larger responsibilities.

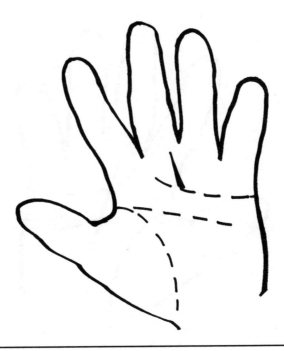

A tiresome and difficult old age

A new career line that appears above the head line indicates a hard life, in which the person will have to work and toil until they die.

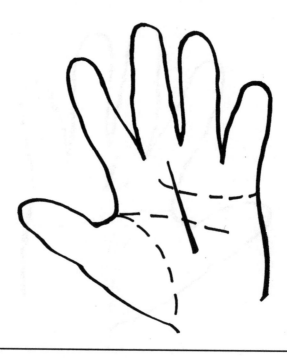

Popularity

When the career line starts with two sidelines, it indicates that the person is well liked. They will have an easy life, receiving a lot of help and attention from family and friends.

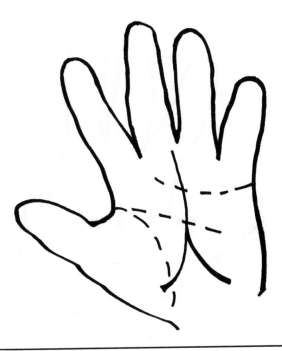

Diligence

When the career line starts from the middle of the life line, it indicates great capability and dedication. It is the sign of a hard-working, goal-getting person.

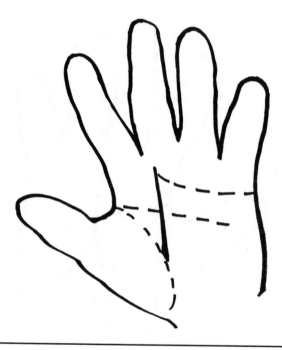

Wealth

When the career line starts at the bottom of the life line and runs upward as shown, it indicates great wealth and lots of support. This person will go far, not only because of their own efforts but because of the help they receive from people close to them.

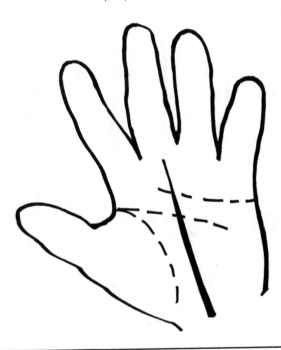

Big and dramatic changes

Several smaller lines that jump out from the life line indicate that the person often changes their mind – ascending lines are positive, descending lines negative. They have difficulty committing themselves to a certain direction and do not know what they really want out of life. They might even make dramatic alterations to their life in terms of career, place of living or partner.

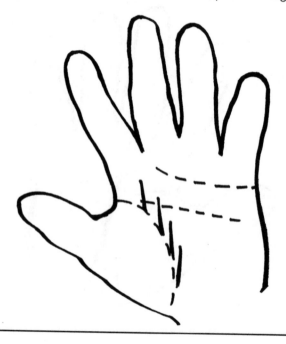

Strong family influence

When the career line is tied to the life line at the base, we are dealing with a person who will be greatly influenced by their family. Often they will follow in the footsteps of their parents, and perhaps share the same means of earning a living.

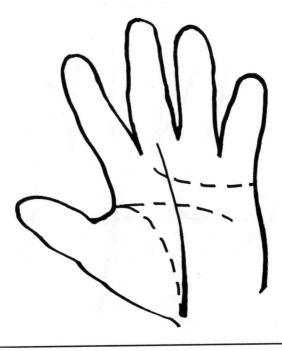

Unlucky circumstances at home and work

A sudden dot on the career line (A) indicates great disturbances at work. A line that arises from point (B) and ends as a dot on the career line shows that someone close to this person could be involved in an accident. A star (C) that appears in the middle of the line is a sign that someone close to this person is trying to trick them.

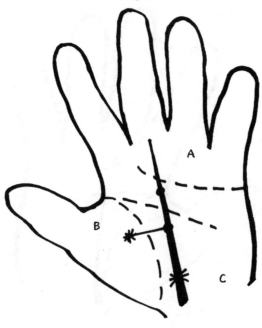

A love affair that ends suddenly

When a sloping line cuts the career line from the mount of the Moon, it indicates a sudden termination of a love affair. It also foretells that the partner is on the point of saying farewell without any form of advance warning.

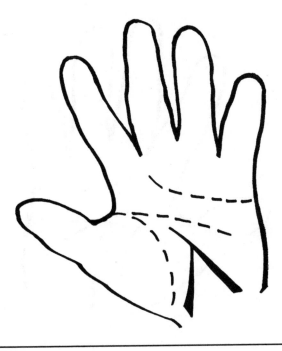

A break in career

A career line that suddenly stops at a point in the middle of the palm indicates an imminent break in career. It could mean that the person ends up drifting without any goal in life.

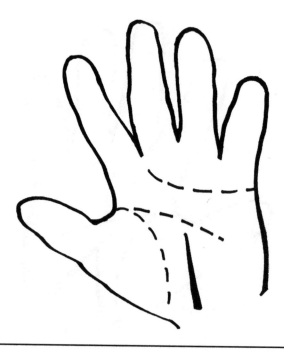

Carelessness
When the career line suddenly stops at the point where it meets the head line, it indicates a setback when the individual is in their mid-thirties. This will be caused by some unforeseen scandal, so the person should be on their guard during this period of their life.

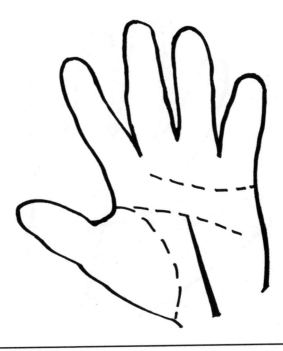

An unlucky involvement in others' affairs

When the career line suddenly stops at the point where it meets the heart line, it indicates an unwise involvement in others' love matters. It means that the individual might be tricked into some deceitful behaviour he or she would have difficulty getting out of, so they should be forewarned.

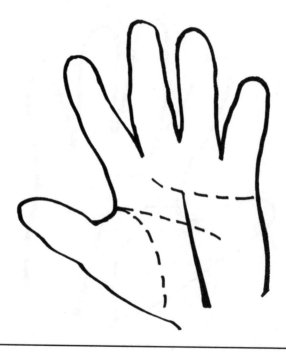

Luck and prosperity

When the career line ends beneath the index finger, it indicates that the person is clearing up their problems and will soon restore their self-confidence. This is a good omen, especially when it appears on the palm of a woman. It shows that she is diplomatic and knows how to associate with surrounding company.

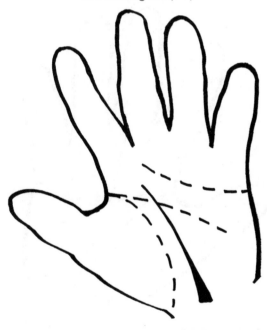

A new career
A career line that suddenly rises from the head line signifies a great career opportunity. It is also evidence of further advancement and the possibility for the individual to make money.

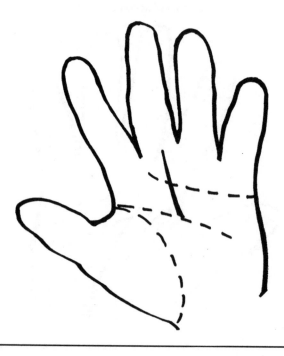

Artistic talents

A career line that emerges from the mount of the Moon is a sign of artistic talents. The most external line (A) indicates talents in the creative arts. The second line (B) shows an open and active person who might be a little too orientated towards sex. The third line (C) suggests a person whose career involves the opposite sex. A lot of famous fashion designers have such a third line. A man with such a configuration will be famous for designing women's clothes; a woman will be good at designing men's clothes.

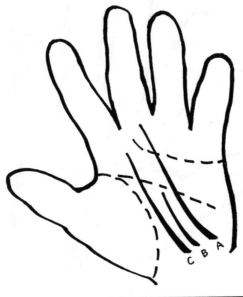

Exaggerated ambition that does not correspond to reality

A career line that runs straight into the first phalanges of the middle finger reveals a person with a misplaced sense of ambition. Unfortunately they do not have the capability to achieve the results they believe they are capable of.

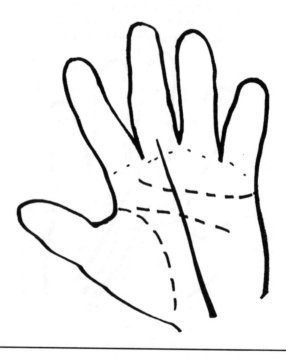

Stubbornness
A long, straight, well-defined career line can be a good sign. However, it can also imply a person who is totally self-occupied and stubborn, so they should try to be more co-operative and diplomatic.

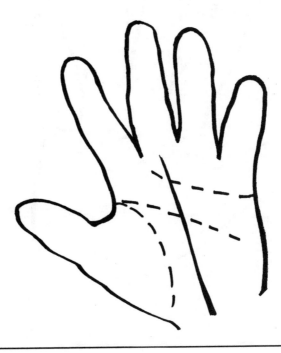

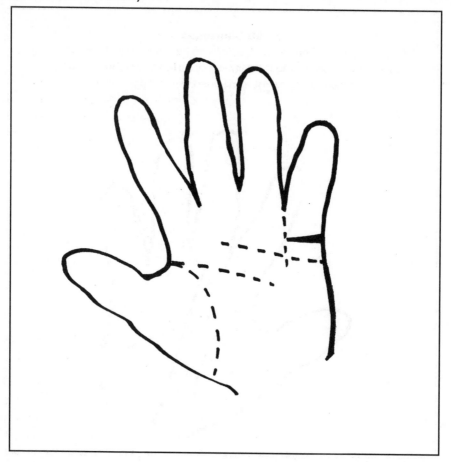

The Love/Marriage Line

This is the small line just beneath the little finger. If it is weak and short, it shows short romantic affairs with no significance. If it is long and distinctive, it indicates a strong love affair and possibly even marriage. An unbroken line with no small, overlapped lines disturbing it shows a healthy and harmonious relationship. A line that is interrupted by smaller lines indicates a marriage that is not functioning well and needs some attention. The space between the heart line and the lower line of the little finger indicates the time span of the course of love. When love/marriage lines occur in this space, it indicates when you will meet someone and how many times you will fall in love. The closer the love/marriage line is to the heart line, the earlier you will fall in love. Here are some analyses of love/marriage line formations and their meanings:

A Don Juan

When there are many fine lines right under the little finger, this indicates a very popular person who is quite a flirt. At times it can be very exciting for such an individual to keep several relationships going, but it can also be rather strenuous and frustrating.

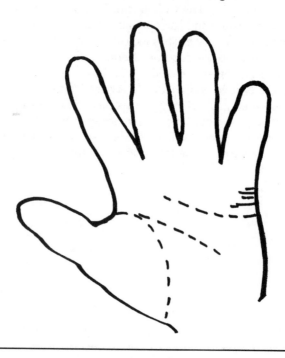

A difficult relationship

When the marriage line bends sharply down towards the direction of the heart line, it suggests a very difficult relationship. If both parties want to carry on, it is vital to improve the mutual understanding and take care of each other's wishes and feelings.

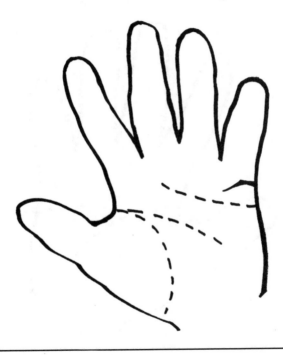

An improved relationship

When the marriage line is gaping, as shown, it reveals a very difficult relationship that is improving every day. Things are once again harmonious and loving, and both parties are doing their best to carry on and make a success of their relationship.

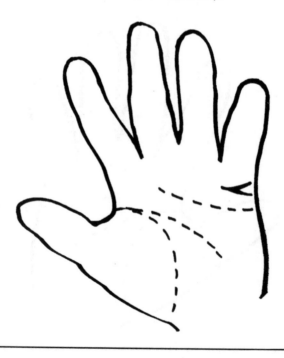

Disagreement

When the marriage line is cut by a needle-sized line, it is a sign of a relationship in distress. Neither of the parties agrees with the other, and there is a lack of intimacy and understanding between them.

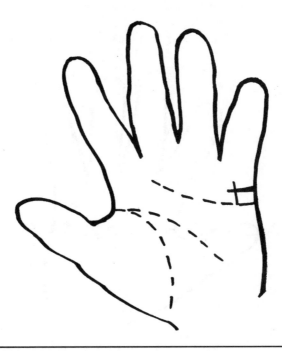

A relationship split in two ways

When the love and marriage line shows a clear line split into two directions, this is a clear indication that the relationship will soon be running into problems. The parties demonstrate that they no longer hold the same interests and goals in life; the bigger the angle between these lines, the larger the difference between the two people involved. Often the relationship will end if the two parties do not nurse it properly. There is also a chance that the relationship will heal itself, however, if the two people involved care deeply enough to do something about it.

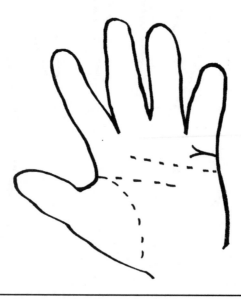

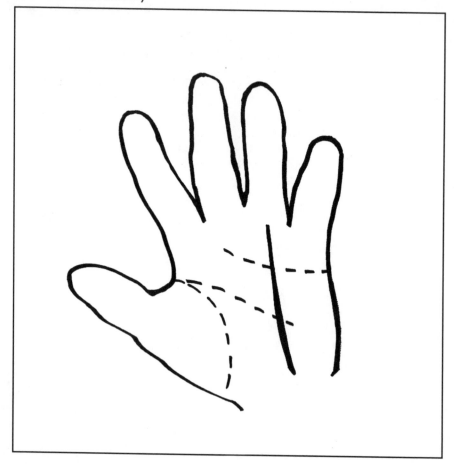

The Success Line
(Sun Line; Line of Apollo)

A success line is an indication of fame and recognition. It is placed just beneath the little finger on the mount of Shen (mount of Apollo). The longer and more well marked it is, the more fame and recognition the person will receive. And if it appears together with the career line, then life is smiling upon you. Whatever you choose to do, you will succeed with great ease. Creative types such as actors, artists and writers would have such formations on their palms.

Appreciation and respect from close ones

When the success line suddenly turns up on the heart line, it is a sign of respect for what you have achieved. This is a positive omen that luck and happiness will remain with you.

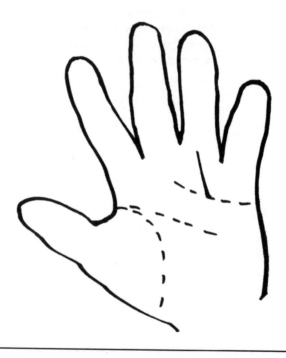

Self-fulfilment

This is a lucky line formation that often appears together with a good career line, in which case the person will reach the top in whatever they choose to do. This line can be very strong, as indicated in the illustration, or it can be weaker or shorter. The longer and deeper the line, the better – it indicates someone with extraordinary will power who will go far in their search for fame and fortune.

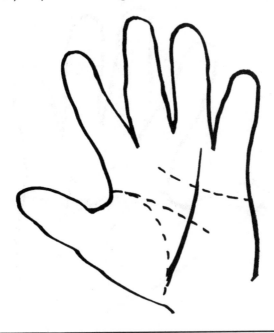

Too much ambition

If a line is cutting the success line, the person will have to think twice before embarking on new projects. This formation indicates they are exaggerating their capabilities, which will win them more enemies than friends. The person should be extra careful in order to avoid indulgence and scandal.

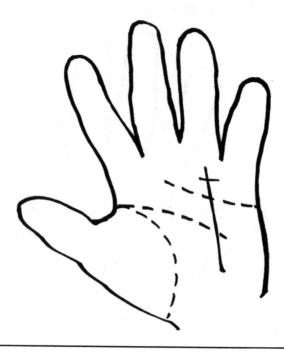

Too many irons in the fire and far-off success

When there are many small lines just beneath the ring finger, it is a sign of a person with too many irons in the fire. It is vital for them to think things over before going ahead with new projects. It would be better for them to concentrate on present commitments.

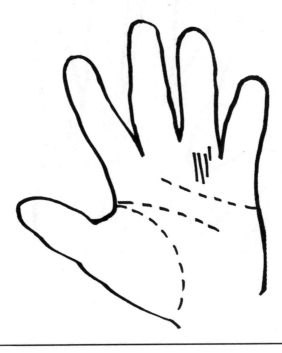

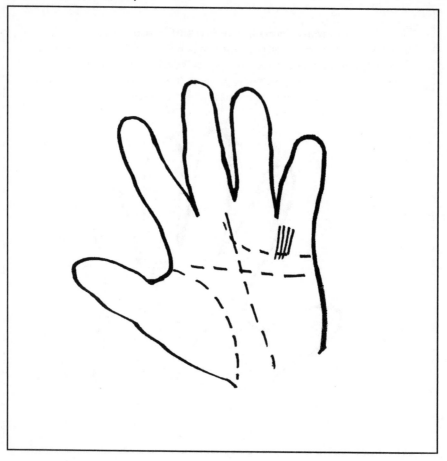

The Money Lines

The many fine lines that appear on the mount under the little finger
are the money lines, which indicate whether or not you are
successful in your work. If they appear, you will have the golden
touch of King Midas.

MARKINGS OF THE PALM

The **star** is a very favourable sign on any part of the palm, often offering reinforcement to another feature. However, you should analyse the entire hand first before adding a positive meaning to the attributes of the palm.

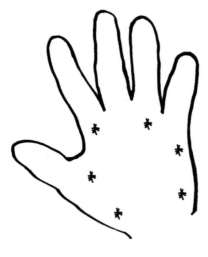

A star on the mount of Ken (Venus)

This is the marking of conquering love. The greatest lovers, including the irresistible Don Juan, and powerful seductresses all bear this marking.

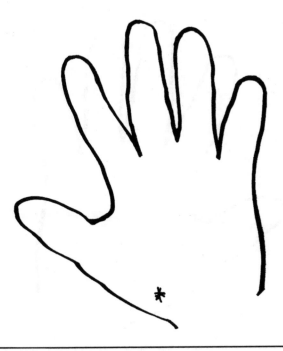

A star on the mount of Zheng (Mars)
This denotes military honours. Defence ministers often have this marking.

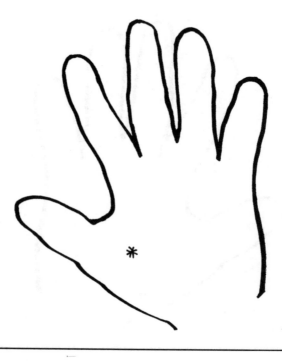

A star on the mount of Xun (Jupiter)
This is a reinforcing sign at all times. If the hand is a good and practical hand,
it is a sign of a person with leadership quality.

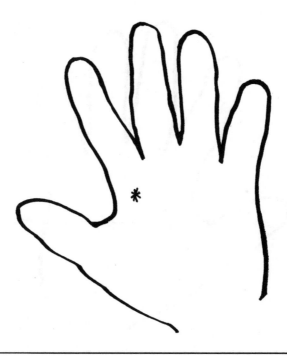

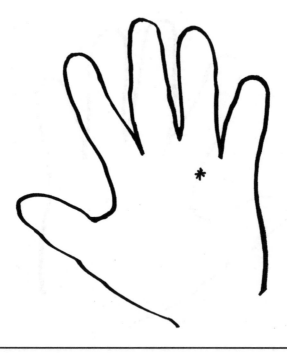

A star on the mount of Li (Apollo)
This denotes great brilliance and recognition for the person.

A star on the mount of Shen (Mercury)

This shows talent and success in science late in life. It is often found on great scientists who ultimately gain recognition.

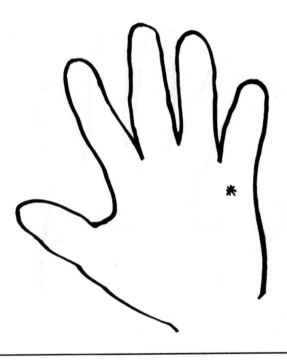

A star on the mount of Tui (Mars)
This suggests military honours late in life. Often generals would have such a marking.

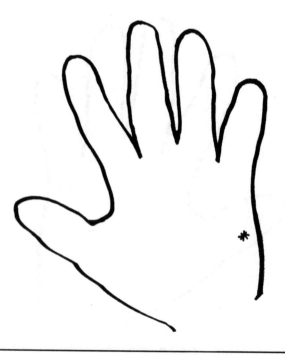

A star on the mount of Chien (Luna)
This is a sign of an incredible, perhaps excessive, imagination.
Often it denotes the borderline between imaginative genius and insanity.

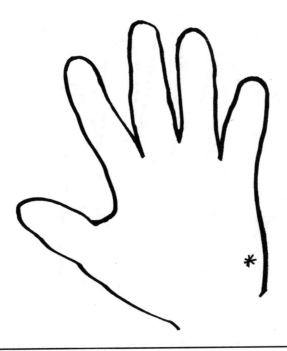

The triangle
The **triangle** is always a favourable trait.
However, it must be clearly marked and not made up by occasional lines.

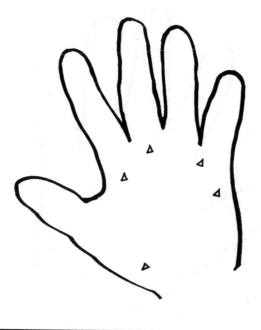

A triangle on the mount of Ken (Venus)
This denotes great power in love and sex.

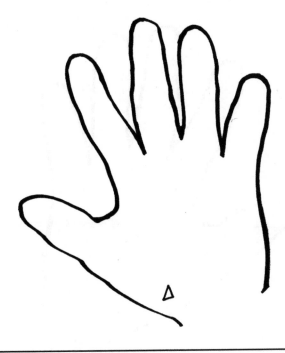

A triangle on the mount of Xun (Jupiter)
This is a sign of a great organizer and a highly successful leader.

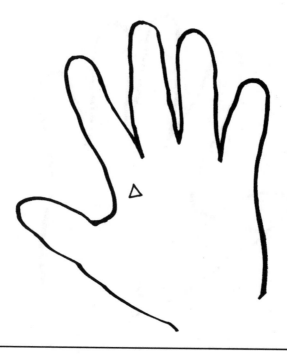

A triangle on the mount of Li (Apollo)
This belongs to a master in the arts, a self-assured creator or an expert musician.

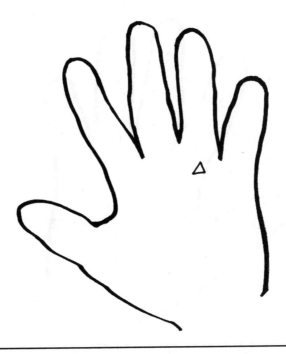

A triangle on the mount of Shen (Mercury)
This indicates an expert in their particular field – a top athlete, or leading financier, for example.

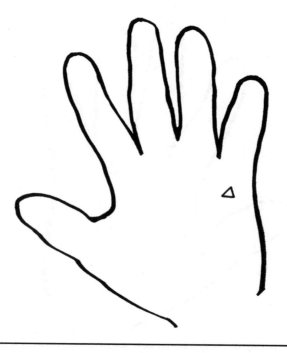

A triangle on the mount of Tui (Mars)

This is a sign of great courage and knowledge in exploration and warfare.

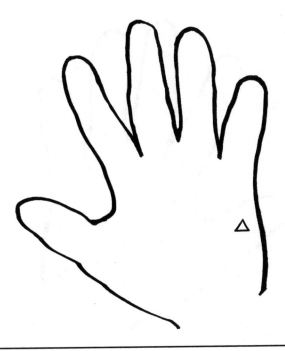

A triangle on the mount of Chien (Luna)

This represents the highest level of imagination, an extremely positive marking for a writer of fiction.

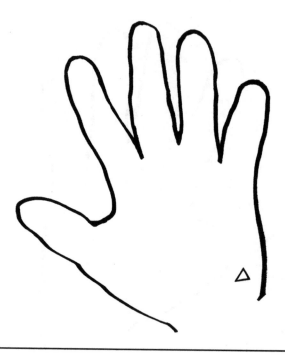

Vertical or horizontal lines on the mounts
All **vertical** lines reinforce the hand, all **horizontal** lines weaken it.
Vertical lines running along the life line, career line and sun line reinforce
these lines; all horizontal lines crossing them denote hindrances.

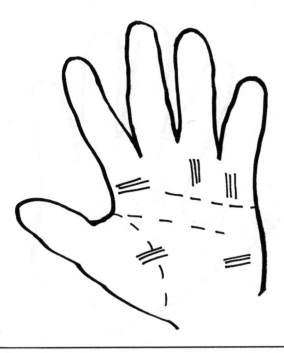

Vertical lines on the mount of Xun (Jupiter)
These indicate success for a political, military, or religious leader.

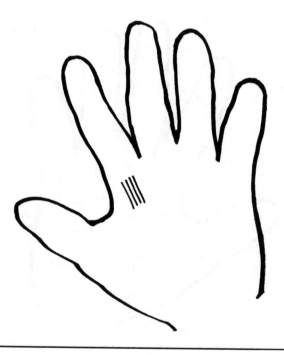

Vertical lines on the mount of Li (Apollo)
These often reinforce the sun line and denote success in the creative arts in later life.

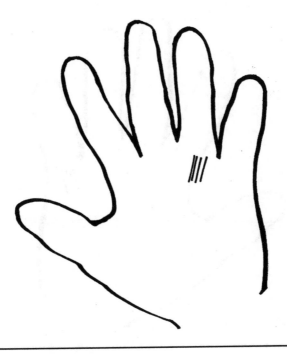

Vertical lines on the mount of Shen (Mercury)

These often reinforce the money lines, denoting success in business.

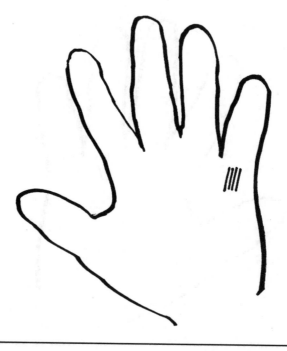

Vertical lines on the mount of Tui (Luna)

These can often be confused with the line of intuition and the line of health, but they indicate travel.

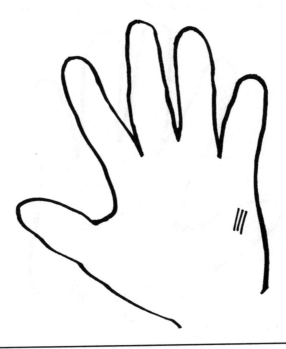

Vertical lines on the mount of Tui, Zheng and Hum

The mounts of Zheng and Tui are related to family matters, while the mount of Hum is connected to one's property, including matters concerning all kinds of technical equipment. Vertical lines are positive, strengthening the person's ability to handle technical equipment; at the same time, it is an indication that he or she is helpful towards others.

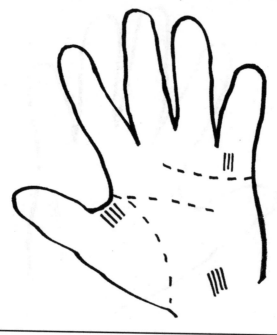

Horizontal lines on the mount of Ken (Venus)
If these cross the life line, they are considered to be a forewarning
of negative events.

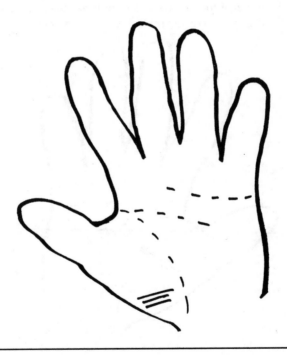

Horizontal lines on the mount of Zheng

Lines appearing on the mount of Zheng are connected to family matters or relationships with one's siblings. If the lines are good – i.e. they have no breaks and do not cut through any main lines (such as the life line, head line or career line on the palm), then they are positive and have the right influence. However, if they cut these lines or break them, it is a sign that siblings will create problems for the individual.

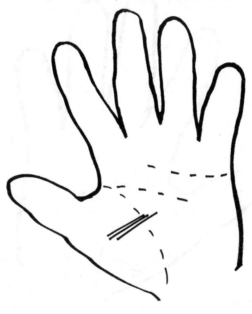

Horizontal lines on the mount of Xun (Jupiter)

These belong to someone who does not want to follow a leadership or religious dictum.

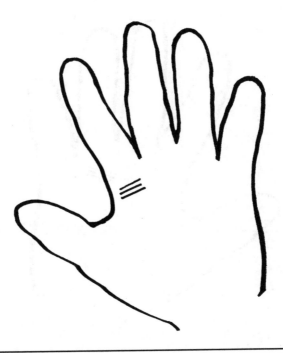

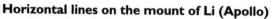

Horizontal lines on the mount of Li (Apollo)
These signal negative forces in the field of creativity.

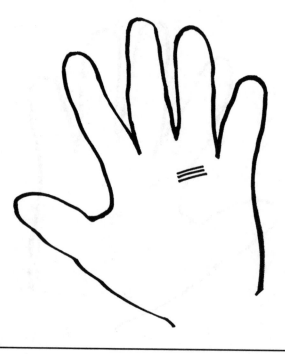

Horizontal lines on the mount of Shen (Mercury)
These indicate negative influences for athletes, businessmen and anyone who wants to obtain success that will be difficult to accomplish.

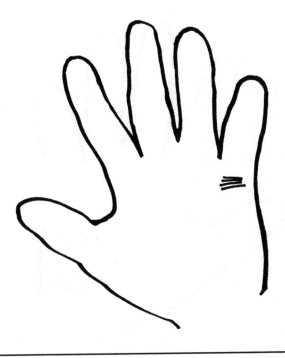

Horizontal lines on the mount of Chien (Luna)
These indicate success in travelling, as long as they are not broken.

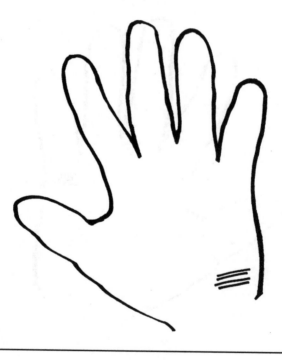

A mystical cross on the mount of Xun (Jupiter) and the Ming Tang (belt of Mars)

The mount of Xun signifies power, and the **cross** is often linked to mystical and paranormal qualities. The appearance of a cross on this mount is a sure sign of someone with strong psychic power.

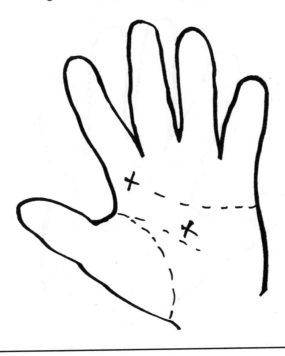

Squares on any part of the palm
These are preservation marks, safeguarding against trouble of any kind.

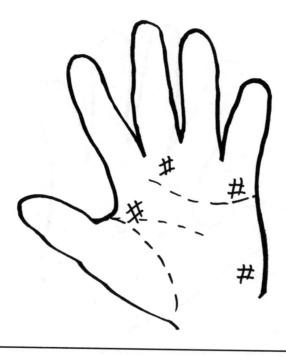

All four major lines in the palm form a letter 'M'

The most important lines of the palm are the life line, the head line, the love/marriage line and the career line. The best formation is when all four lines are linked together to form the letter 'M', since it shows their strongest starting and ending points. As explained earlier, the longer the lines, the better.

FINGERS AND THUMB TYPE

The thumb

The thumb indicates the will and the way to make decisions. If the thumb is strong and well formed, it is a sign of good health, excellent manners and fine leadership capabilities. Men with well-formed thumbs are often very good lovers.

The index finger

The index finger indicates power and ambition. If the finger is thick and strong, this denotes a person with strong determination and the willingness to obtain power. Good politicians and business leaders often have strong index fingers. Such people are likely to succeed in anything that involves dealing with people.

The middle finger

The middle finger denotes conscience and moral standards. If the finger is thick, strong and very straight, it is a sign of someone with a good conscience. But if it is excessively long, it is a sign of someone who ponders a lot and prefers to do things in their own way.

The ring finger

The ring finger denotes the artistic side of a person. If the finger is strong, thick and rather long, it reveals a person who comes from a wealthy family. However, if it is excessively long and thick, it reveals a person who is very fond of gambling.

The little finger

The little finger represents how well someone mingles and socializes with people around them. If the finger is thick and strong, it reveals a person who is diplomatic, a good conversationalist and well liked. A good little finger should at least reach up to the second phalanges of the ring finger. If it is shorter, it shows a very timid person. Some women with very short little fingers may even experience problems becoming pregnant.

Fingertip Type

There are commonly four types of fingertip shapes – pointed, round, spatulate and square – and each reveals its own special character and even destiny.

Pointed

These people have artistic, romantic and sensitive natures. They can be diplomatic and are fond of making new friends. They will also be extremely idealistic, with little understanding of the value of money. Wealth is not important to them.

Round

These people are sharp and intelligent, and often lack the patience to do things properly. A lot of artistic people are born with such fingers. They will have to learn to be patient and take one step at a time in order to be successful.

Square

These people show great awareness when dealing with a range of matters. They are alert, careful and constructive. They tend to have excellent administrative abilities, which means they have the ability to go far in any kind of organizational work and to become both rich and famous.

Spatulate fingers
These people are very independent, with a taste for travel and outdoor life.
They are pragmatic and ambitious to reach their goals in life.

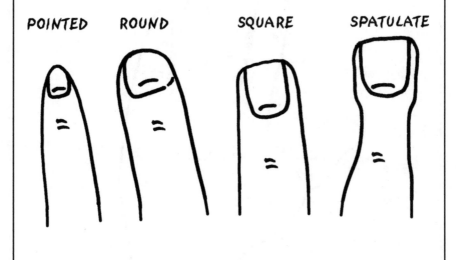

POINTED   ROUND   SQUARE   SPATULATE

GAPS BETWEEN THE FINGERS

Gap between the index finger and middle finger

This denotes a person who does not want to be controlled by others. However, they are also quite smart, so they should be capable of obtaining wealth and fame without any difficulty.

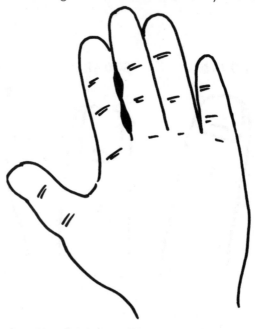

Gap between the middle finger and the ring finger

This denotes a person who prefers to be independent and free. However, the individual will have to work for this kind of lifestyle, as he or she may be prone to drifting without any real goals in life.

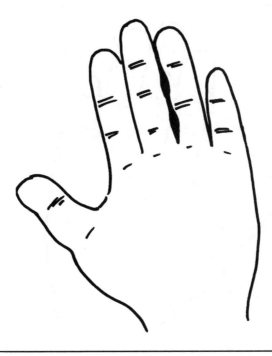

Gap between the ring finger and little finger

This characterizes someone who has their own ideas and prefers to run their show alone. It also indicates a very artistic and creative person who knows what they want. They should be able to obtain wealth and fame without too much effort.

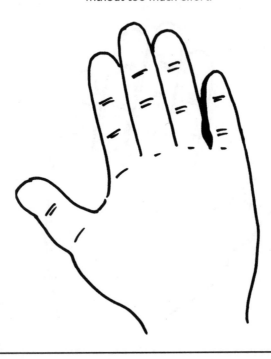

Gaps between all the fingers

This is a sign of someone who is careless with their spending and has an untraditional style of living. They are very optimistic, but at times they will be in economic trouble because of their lack of money sense.

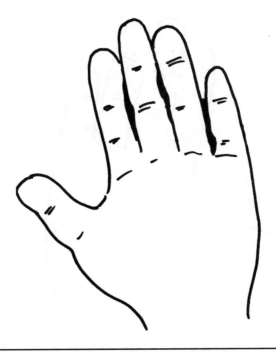

No gap between the fingers
This denotes a person who is careful, earth-bound and a keen conservationist. Everything must be thought of and nothing will be wasted. This person will go far in their search for fame and fortune.

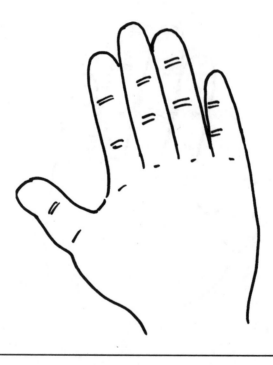

Angle between the thumb and the index finger
is wider than 90 degrees

This shows an adventurous and generous nature. Often it is sign of a very enterprising person who has to spend money before reaping big rewards.

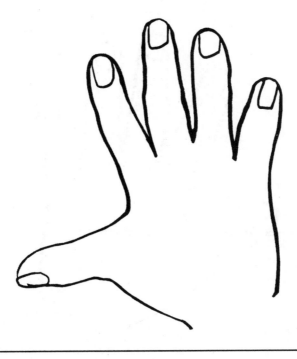

Angle between the thumb and the index finger is less than 60 degrees

This denotes a very cautious person who is careful with their money. But they are no good at making money, and they might even lose their friends because of their selfishness.

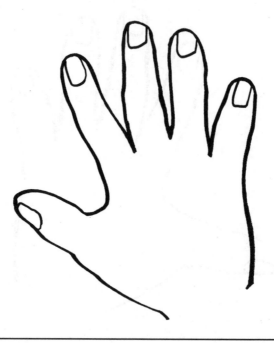

FINGERPRINTS

All fingers have whorls

A **whorl** is a complete circle and often indicates a person who is fastidious and a good administrator. When all the fingers have whorls, it shows strong self-confidence, independence and stubbornness. All these qualities will of course influence the person's destiny, so it is vital that they are aware of this sign. Perhaps they need to be more flexible and diplomatic.

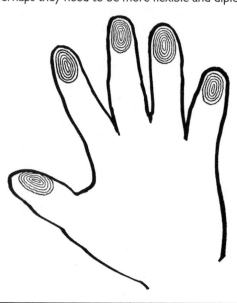

Only the thumb has a whorl

This is a good omen, indicating a gentle, diplomatic person with many talents. It is a sign of strong will power and a strong physique. However, such a person usually tends to be impatient.

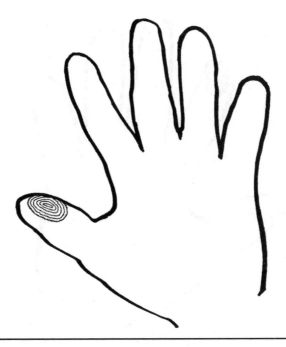

Only the index finger has a whorl

This person is good at socializing, but they tend to be an opportunist and often change their mind along the way. These negative tendencies might bring difficulties if they do not change their attitude and approach.

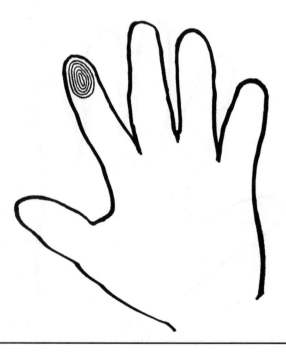

Only the middle finger has a whorl

This belongs to a person with high goals in life, but the goals might be difficult to reach. They must learn to be realistic and keep both the feet on the ground – then they will go far.

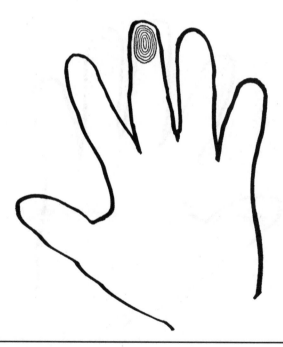

Only the ring finger has a whorl

This person will achieve a lot at an early stage of life. They will be a good leader, and if they know how to be patient they will achieve much more.

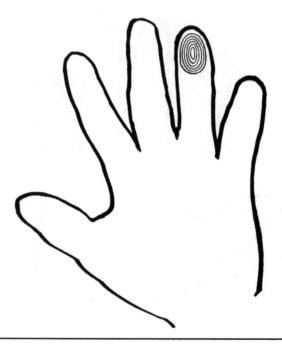

Only the little finger has a whorl
This also shows a gentle, pleasant person with many talents. They will be easily noticed and people will always be willing to help them. They will progress far in their career, but first they must learn to trust people.

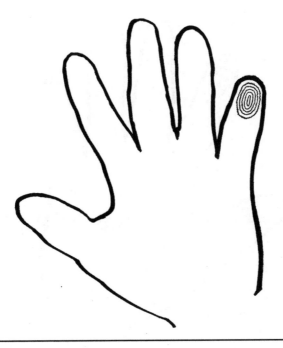

Only the thumb and the index finger have whorls

This indicates a sociable person with great tolerance and flexibility. They tend to be soft-hearted and will often take on others' problems without thinking. They will have to learn not to trust everybody they encounter.

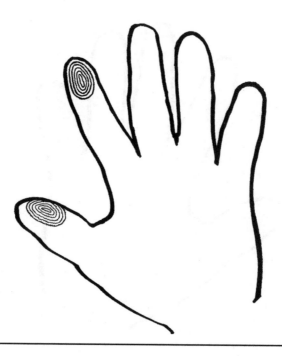

Only the thumb and the middle finger have whorls

This is a sign of a restless person. If they are willing to work long and hard, they will succeed, and are likely to become widely recognized.

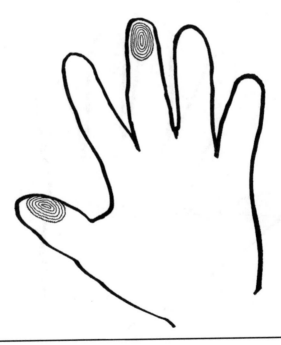

Only the thumb and the ring finger have whorls

This person will have to work hard in order to get by. It is vital that they realize this and get things started early in life. As they get older, the chances increase of them obtaining a high position, becoming rich and even becoming famous.

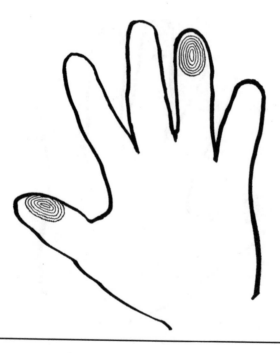

Only the thumb and the little finger have whorls

This shows someone who is very vocal, so they should choose work that involves communicating with others. They will be sure to do well in their chosen field. They are likely to be a top salesman and have excellent communication and marketing skills.

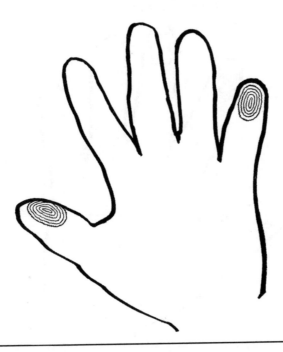

Only the index finger and middle finger have whorls

Such a combination indicates a very straightforward person, someone who prefers not to go around in circles. He or she will attain power and is definitely a leader type. As the index finger stands for power and leadership and the middle finger stands for righteousness, he or she will exert their power in a balanced way.

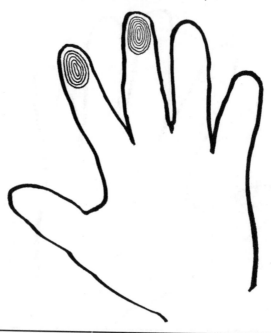

Only the index finger and the ring finger have whorls
This is a sign of a person who is very stubborn and strong-willed and knows exactly what they want in life. With such qualities they are likely to become successful.

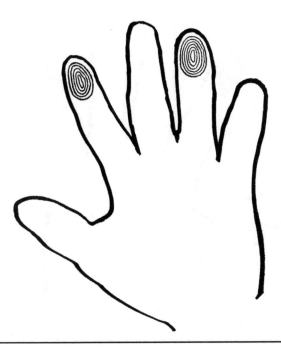

The index finger and the little finger have whorls

This is a sign of someone who is reflective and good at handling things at an early age. If they learn to take things one step at a time, their old age will be prosperous and rewarding.

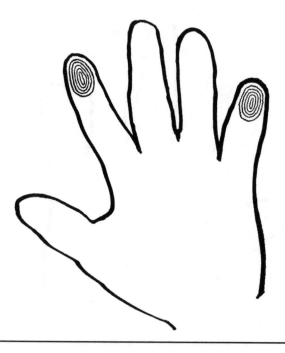

Only the middle finger and the ring finger have whorls.

This combination indicates a righteous and artistic person, as the middle finger stands for good conscience and the ring finger stands for artistic talents. The person will strive to become accomplished in his or her artistic work. Many talented artists that become famous at an early age have such whorls, which are a sign of great success within the arts.

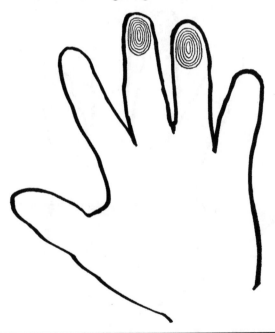

Only the middle finger and the little finger have whorls

This indicates a person with great upheavals and instabilities in life. Sometimes they are on top, other times they are at the bottom. If they know how to take one step at a time, and grasp opportunities when they arise, they will go far.

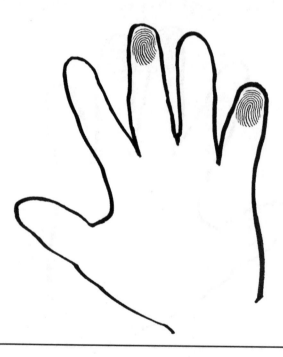

Only the ring finger and the little finger have whorls

This is an indication of someone who is prone to being bad tempered, and may also indicate a weak character. That said, the individual may be very good at work involving good communication skills. However, she or he may well misunderstand the intentions of others and tends to be always on the alert and very suspicious. If the individual can amend these negative qualities, they will succeed in life.

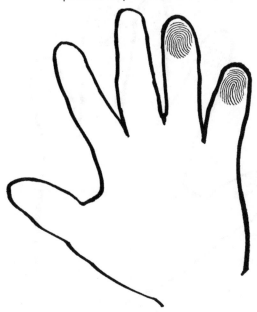

All fingers have loops

Loops are often indications of a person who is artistic and flexible. When all the fingers have loops, it shows a very righteous person with good practical skills. However, they are not very good at socializing, so partnerships – in both the business and the romantic sense – may be problematic.

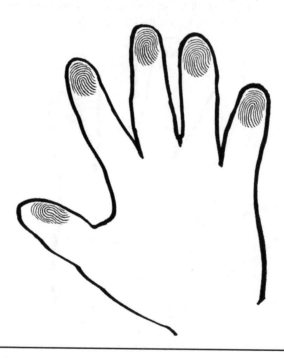

Only the thumb has a loop

This indicates a person who does not care about power and fame. He or she does exactly what pleases them. It is a sign of a rather restless and adventurerous person who will be always on the go. The more positive aspects of this feature are that the individual will also be a pleasant, helpful and freedom-seeking person. He or she will make a lot of friends through life and will never feel lonely.

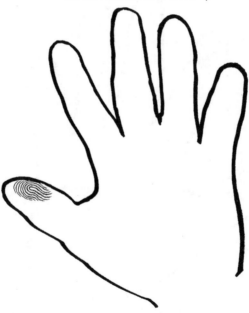

Only the index finger has a loop

This suggests a very righteous person, who tends to be both gentle and self-sacrificing. This makes them unsuitable for business dealing, so they may be more successful in fields connected with education and religion.

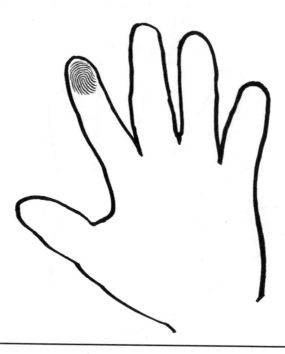

Only the middle finger has a loop

This can demonstrate courage, diligence and a will to work hard. This person will go far and people will always be supportive towards their ideas. However, they might also be someone who is revengeful and does not forgive easily. If they are willing to do something about this negative aspect, life will be much easier for them at a later stage.

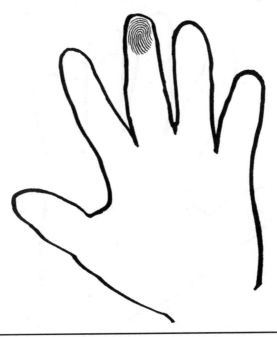

Only the ring finger has a loop
This reveals a gentle and diplomatic person. They will easily progress in any career they choose to follow, and will be supported and helped by colleagues. Their old age will be prosperous in every sense.

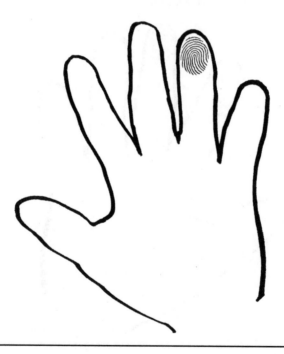

Only little finger has a loop

Definitely not the sign of a good business person. He or she likes to spend money and has difficulty in saving it. On the positive side, if the career line and money lines are good, then he or she will be able to afford anything they want. This is also a sign of a very generous person who is willing to share wealth with friends and relatives.

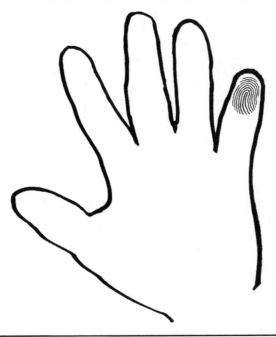

Only the thumb and the index finger have loops

This person is hard-working and productive, but might be somewhat indecisive and impatient. This combination is also a sign of a particular weakness: the individual may well find that other people take advantage of them – perhaps sexually, or as a result of alcoholic overindulgence. If they can resist such temptations, however, they will succeed in the end.

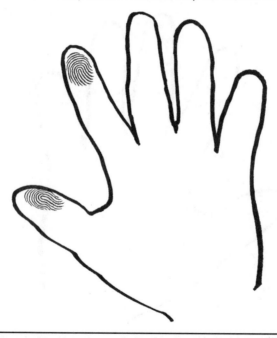

Thumb and middle finger have loops

This is a person who just cares about him- or herself. Such an individual may well have a great heart, and be capable of caring for others, but often he or she prefers to stay alone and get things done independently, without asking anyone for permission. This person seeks a life without too much restriction and is a freedom-loving person.

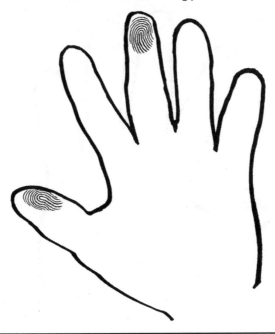

Only the thumb and the ring finger have loops
This is the sign of a simple and earth-bound person who always takes one
step at a time. With that kind of attitude, he/she will proceed well in life.
Fame and wealth will be within their reach.

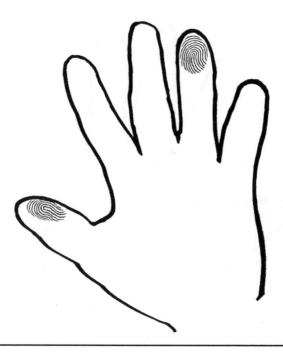

Only the thumb and the little finger have loops

This is the sign of a very righteous person, who tends to be fastidious and self-centred. This will make the individual more enemies than friends.

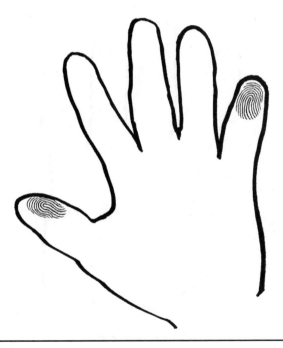

Only the index finger and the middle finger have loops

This indicates a person who is gentle and willing to help others. He or she will be respected and gradually build up a good name for themselves. Though early life will not be easy for such an individual, things will work out in the end, in later years.

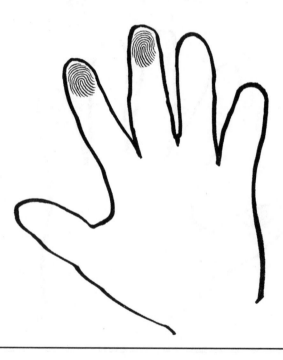

Only the index finger and ring finger have loops

This combination indicates an individual who does not care about being a leader. Such people roam about through life at their own pace and in their own style. They are individuals with a great understanding of the arts, but do nothing much with their talents.

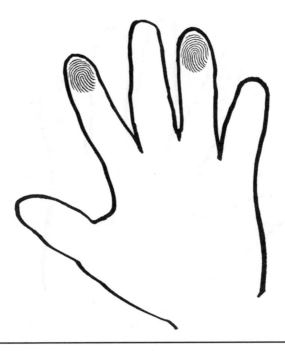

Only the index finger and the little finger have loops

This suggests someone who is tolerant, helpful and a perfect leader type.
They are also very practical and can handle any kind of fine mechanical work.

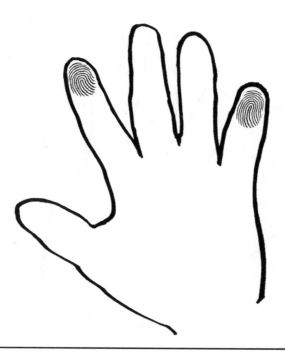

Only the middle finger and the ring finger have loops

This indicates someone with an iron will, but who might lack enough experience to make the right decision about things. Such a combination also suggests someone who does not care much about money. If he or she works hard and is patient, however, things will work out for them.

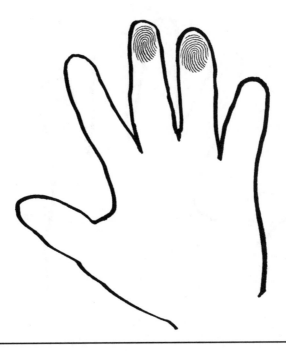

Only the middle finger and the little finger have loops

This is a sign of a person who is great at planning the future. They are especially suited to dealing with risky investments. They can reckon on a prosperous and happy old age.

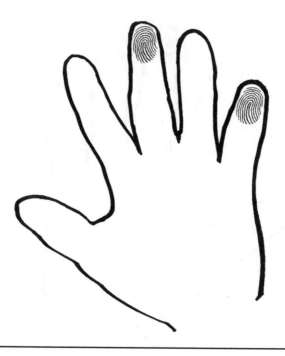

Only the ring finger and little finger have loops

Someone with this combination does not spend too much time developing his or her artistic talents. This person often has great ideas, but they will never be translated into real projects. It is therefore very important that such an individual is trained at an early stage to take things more seriously – certainly, any interest in artistic work will be boosted by such early encouragement.

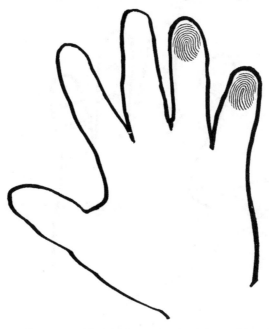

PHALANGES OF THE FINGERS

The Finger Phalanges

The **phalanges** are the bones of the fingers. There are 14 phalanges in the five fingers of each hand: two in the thumb and three in each of the four fingers.

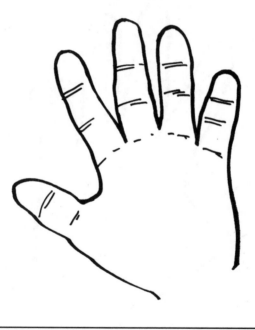

Long phalanges
People with very long finger phalanges are meticulous and thoughtful. This is also a sign of good intelligence.

Short phalanges
People with short phalanges are not very methodical and tend to be rather careless. Although they are not stupid, they fail to think before they leap.

Short, horizontal lines on all the first phalanges
If there are many fine, short lines on the first phalanges of the fingers and the thumb, it is an omen of very poor health. Anyone with such a configuration would benefit from a prompt medical check-up.

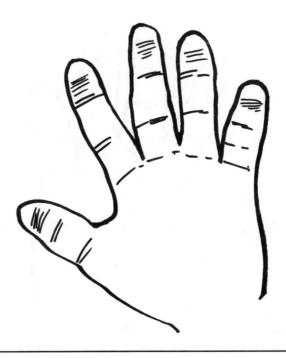

Short, horizontal and wavy lines on all the first phalanges
This indicates bad fortune, or even an imminent accident. The person should be very careful.

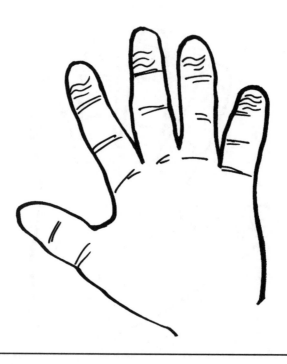

Short and marked vertical lines on all the phalanges
This is a very favourable omen, indicating a person who may enjoy excellent
health and wealth, and even fame. He or she leads a trouble-free life.

Lots of irregular lines on the second phalanges of the thumb

This indicates that the person will be free from any money problems and will have no trouble obtaining fame and fortune. They will have a very strong life line and a marked head line.

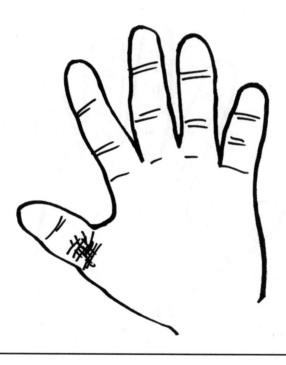

NAILS

The **nails** not only reveal a person's state of health, but also their character and fortune. The most favourable type of nail is one that is only half the length of the fingertip. The little moon – the white, crescent-shaped area of the nail – should at least be one fifth of the nail length. If there are signs of broken or deformed nails, it is a warning of sickness and health problems. In such cases, it would be wise for the individual to go to the doctor to have a check-up.

Good overall nail shape and texture

This is a nail that reveals good health, and a strong, open and loving character. The person will be well loved and will have a successful career.

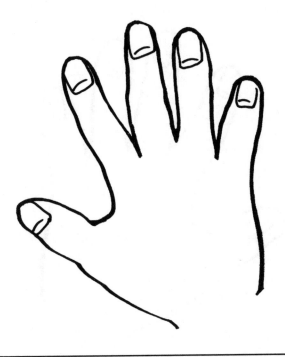

Long nail

An artistic and sentimental person is likely to have such nails. They can be somewhat timid and are most likely an introvert. They may also experience recurring lung and throat problems.

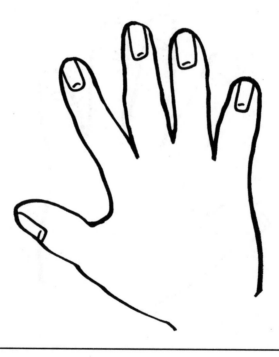

Short nail

This indicates people with a clear mind, who are willing to work hard to reach their goals. However, they are too stubborn, which may make them unpopular with people. A short nail also foretells a person with a weak heart, who is likely to suffer a heart attack. If this nail occurs on a female, it can often mean problems with the ovaries, leading to infertility.

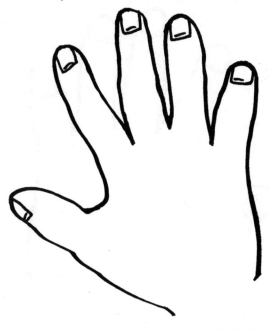

Wide nail
This indicates a person who is open, loves to be in focus and can be very communicative indeed. He/she loves to be in charge – however, he/she might be rather too self-confident. Such an individual is often a pioneer in many things, but at the end tends to lack the final drive and touch to complete work properly.

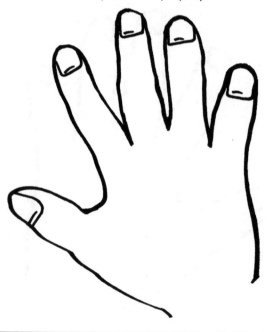

Narrow nail
This is a sign of a person who is always on the alert and very indecisive – they never manage to decide what direction to take. They may be good at starting things, but they will never be able to complete them and they will leave things in a mess.

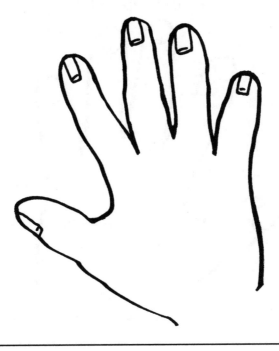

Round nail

This belongs to a person who is open-minded, caring and diplomatic, but they might be too indecisive and often change their mind. This person can be very successful if they know their weaknesses and do something about them. An eventual alliance with someone who is stronger in will and mind will help them to get along in life.

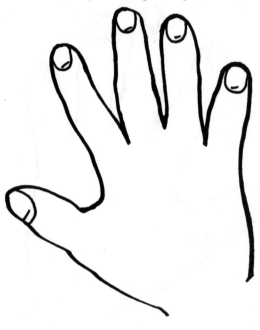

Long and narrow nail

This is a sign of strong idealism and – at times – great sensitivity. This person can be rather moody and difficult to understand. Females with such a nail type will have a weaker bone structure, and it may be worthwhile for them to check that they are receiving enough calcium from their food in order to avoid bone problems such as osteoporosis.

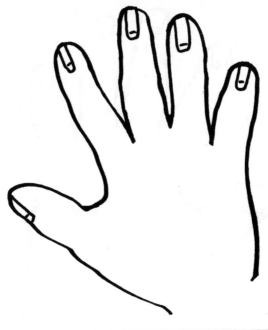

Triangular nail

This indicates a rebellious and suspicious person, who may even be a bit psychotic. They will not be easy for others to understand, and may well experience great difficulties as they proceed through life.

The only way out is for them to curb these negative qualities and try to learn to develop a more positive attitude.

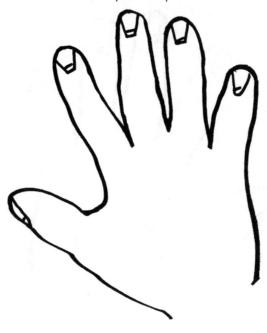

Nail with perpendicular lines and small dots

This is a very bad sign, suggesting digestion problems that are often brought about by heavy smoking. It may be wise for the individual concerned to see a doctor and arrange for a medical check-up.

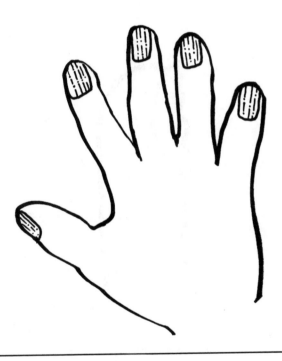

Nail with a wavy appearance

A nail with a wavy appearance, as seen from the side, indicates intestinal problems. Often it is a sign of heavy haemorrhoids.

Nail with perpendicular stripes

This is a sign of poor health. The person will tend to be very tense and nervous, and may even have potentially psychotic tendencies. He or she may well benefit from a thorough medical examination.

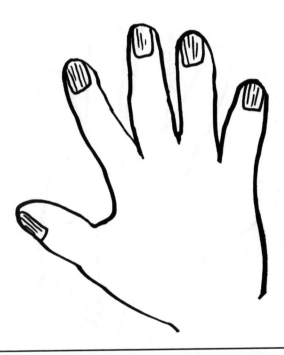

LINES OF THE WRIST

Three or more lines on the wrist

This is an indication of health and good fortune if the lines are marked and have good colour. Otherwise, the contrary is true.

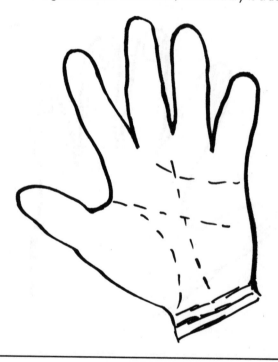

The upper line on the wrist is arched

This shows a person who is having problems with their reproductive system, which often leads to fertility problems. It may be advisable for them to seek advice from a doctor.

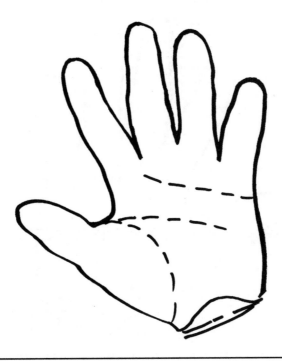

A cross is shown on one of the wrist lines
This signals a person who will have a difficult time when young, though things will become easier for them once they get older. In later life they may well become wealthy and perhaps even well known.

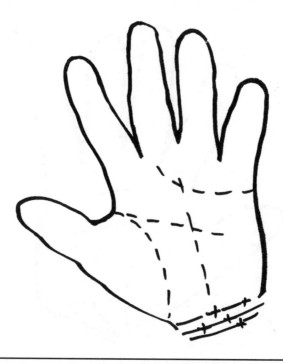

Wrist lines that look like chains

Strenuous times lie ahead for this person. They will have to work hard through life because, for them, nothing is free of charge.

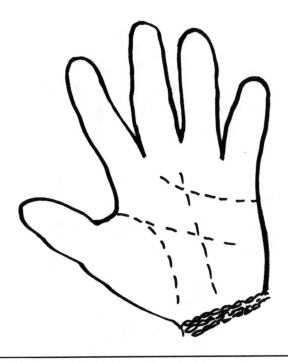

One or several stars on the wrist lines
This is a very good omen, denoting the person will come across a fortune and become wealthy and perhaps even famous.

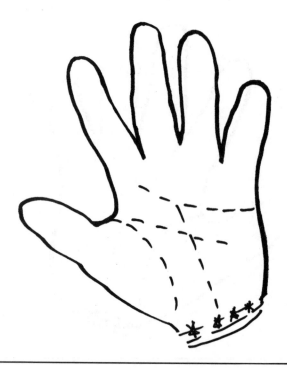

The wrist lines form a triangle at the base of the palm

This indicates that the person may well become rich and famous because of their talents and hard work. It could even be an omen of a forthcoming piece of good luck, such as a lottery prize.

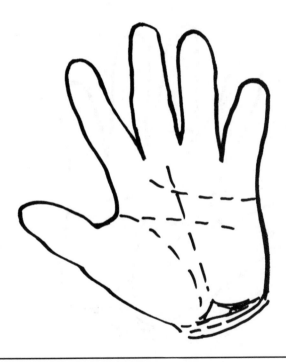

The wrist lines form a triangle with a star in it
This is suggestive of immense wealth and fortune. The person is likely to succeed in whatever they choose to do.

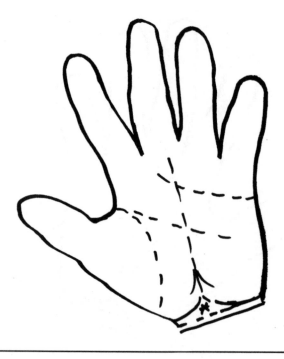

FAMOUS PEOPLE AND THEIR PALMS

Charlie Chaplin
Born in London, England, 16 April 1889

Film actor and director Charlie Chaplin directed and starred in many silent comedy films. He usually played a bowler-hatted tramp, a trademark character that became instantly recognizable around the globe and brought laughter to millions.

Chaplin's head line formed a very sharp angle with his life line, which reached straight down to the mount of the Moon. This formation reveals a person who has a lot of dreams and visions. He also had a very strong career line, which stretched to the middle finger with a very marked triangle at the end. This indicates that Chaplin managed to realize most of his dreams, and that he brought much joy to the world around him. However, the marriage line was somewhat disordered, a reflection of his many stormy relationships.

Roald Amundsen
Born in Borge, Norway, 16 July 1872

Polar explorer Roald Amundsen was one of the bravest men in history. Well known for his strong will and resourcefulness, Amundsen famously led the first expedition to reach the South Pole successfully. Unfortunately his last trip – to the North Pole, in order to save his friend and fellow explorer Umberto Nobile – ended in tragedy. Amundsen's aeroplane is believed to have crashed during the journey to the North Pole; he never returned.

Amundsen's head line was separated from his life line – a sign of strong will and bravery. His head line was also very long, which indicates an intelligent and enterprising person. The line of travel, connected to the life line, was very marked and rather long, which shows a very adventurous person. The same line also ended with a star, indicating that Amundsen was willing to sacrifice anything in order to reach his destination.

Thomas Alva Edison
Born in Milan, Ohio, United States, 11 February 1847

Thomas Edison is one of the world's most ingenious and prolific inventors, who managed to patent more than 1,000 discoveries. He became especially famous because of one unique invention – the incandescent electric lightbulb, which revolutionized our daily lives.

Edison's head line was strong and marked, indicating high intelligence with a desire to do research. In the middle of his palm there was a big star, which indicates fame and recognition.

Albert Einstein
Born in Ulm, Germany, 14 March 1879

One of the greatest scientists of the twentieth century, physicist Albert Einstein was a person with great vision and high intelligence. His groundbreaking Theory of Relativity, which explains how gravity and motion affect time and space, is still widely used to this day.

Einstein's head line was long and travelled down to the mount of the Moon – a sign of fantasy and visions. He also had a well-marked triangle on the mount of the Moon, which indicates he was always looking for answers. Just beneath his ring finger were three small lines – a sign of success and recognition for his work.

Sigmund Freud
Born in Freiberg, Moravia (now part of the Czech Republic), 6 May 1856

Neurologist and psychotherapist Sigmund Freud pioneered new techniques for understanding human behaviour, including psychoanalysis. His theories are known the world over, and his working methods have helped thousands of people with mental problems. He was fond of using alternative methods to treat his patients – with very good results – and he was the first psychologist to apply hypnosis and palmistry to diagnose mental sickness.

Freud had a career line running towards the index finger, with a subsidiary line ending just beneath the ring finger, indicating success. He also had three small lines on the mount of the Sun, indicating fame.

Greta Garbo
Born in Stockholm, Sweden, 18 September 1905

Greta Garbo was one of the most glamorous and popular stars of the motion pictures of the 1920s and 1930s. Her great beauty and her skilful interpretation of great film roles made her famous and well loved the world over.

The fine half circle around the lowest part of Garbo's index finger was particularly prominent. This is a sign of a truly gifted film actress.

Marie Curie
Born in Warsaw, Poland, 7 November 1867

Nobel Prize-winning physicist Marie Curie and her husband, Pierre Curie, won fame for their discovery of radium, which was used as a source of radiation in radiotherapy. Curie spent the rest of her life on research and combat against cancer.

Curie had a strong and marked head line – a sign of high intelligence. Her palm also had an arch line that stretched from the mount of the Moon towards the mount of Mercury – an indication that her intuition would bring her great success in her profession.

The marriage line was broken, a reflection of the fact that her relationship with Pierre did not last very long. He died after a car accident in 1906.

APPENDIX

Case Study

Chinese palmistry has been widely used for thousands of years. The application of palmistry is wide and varied, but one thing is certain: it can be used to prevent many unhappy incidents. I have found Chinese palmistry to be extremely accurate – a fact that can be confirmed by many of my clients.

There is one particular case I recall. A Danish girl once came to me to have her fortune told. She was working as a nurse on board the *MS Scandinavian Star*, commuting between Norway and Denmark. From her palm I could tell that she would find herself in the middle of a dramatic accident very soon, and since she was working on board the ferry, I asked her to be extra alert. I assured her that she would manage, whatever happened. And off she went.

That very weekend a fire broke out on board the *MS Scandinavian Star*, and the Danish girl was the last survivor to be rescued. She later revealed to me that what I had told her had meant a lot to her, and it was those words that had kept her alive, even though she was poisoned by gas and smoke during the fire. She managed to keep herself conscious until the rescue team picked her up.

ABOUT THE AUTHOR

Henning Hai Lee Yang was born in the Year of the Ox and he says that he is doomed to work hard all the time, like so many others born in the same astrological sign. He has always been interested in the art of Chinese fortune-telling and can trace his family tree back over a thousand years to the legendary sage Yang Chiu Pun, one of China's most famous fortune-tellers.

Henning Hai Lee Yang's father, Yang Leong Fok, ran a successful business recruiting Chinese seamen for Norwegian shipping companies from 1949 to 1966, and thus brought the family into contact with Norway. Yang Leong Fok understood the importance of knowing the men around him and could manage thousands of seamen in their work.

Henning Hai Lee Yang was educated as a business economist and marine engineer, and is currently working towards a doctorate in philosophy. Since 1987 he has devoted himself to a highly successful career in Chinese fortune-telling and has written more than 38 books on the subject. He specializes in Chinese and Western astrology, face and hand reading, I Ching and Feng Shui. Based in Oslo, he frequently appears on radio and television programmes worldwide, and is a regular contributor to many newspapers and magazines.

If you wish to reach Henning Hai Lee Yang, his contact details are as follows:
The Master of Chinese Fortune-telling
Henning Hai Lee Yang
Brugaten 1, 0186 Oslo, Norway
Tel: (+) 47 22 17 72 50   Fax: (+) 47 22 17 05 42
E-mail: yangz@yangz.com   Web site: www.yangz.com